MANAGING *for* VALUE

MANAGING for VALUE

(THIRD EDITION)

S.S. Iyer
Management Consultant
and
Certified Value Engineering Specialist

NEW AGE MANAGEMENT

An Imprint of

NEW AGE INTERNATIONAL (P) LIMITED, PUBLISHERS

New Delhi • Bangalore • Chennai • Cochin • Guwahati • Hyderabad
Jalandhar • Kolkata • Lucknow • Mumbai • Ranchi
Visit us at **www.newagepublishers.com**

Published by New Age International (P) Ltd., Publishers
First Edition: 2002
Third Edition: 2009
Reprint: 2010

Branches:

- No. 37/10, 8th Cross (Near Hanuman Temple), Azad Nagar, Chamrajpet, **Bangalore**- 560 018.Tel.: (080) 26756823, Telefax: 26756820 E-mail: bangalore@newagepublishers.com
- 26, Damodaran Street, T. Nagar, **Chennai**- 600 017. Tel.: (044) 24353401, Telefax: 24351463, E-mail: chennai@newagepublishers.com
- CC-39/1016, Carrier Station Road, Ernakulam South, **Cochin**- 682 016. Tel.: (0484) 2377004, Telefax: 4051303, E-mail: cochin@newagepublishers.com
- Hemsen Complex, Mohd. Shah Road, Paltan Bazar, Near Starline Hotel, **Guwahati**- 781 008, Tel.: (0361) 2513881, Telefax: 2543669 E-mail: guwahati@newagepublishers.com
- No. 105, 1st Floor, Madhiray Kaveri Tower, 3-2-19, Azam Jahi Road, Nimboliadda, **Hyderabad**- 500 027. Tel.: (040) 24652456, Telefax: 24652457 E-mail:hyderabad@newagepublishers.com
- RDB Chambers (Formerly Lotus Cinema)106A, 1st Floor, S.N. Banerjee Road, **Kolkata**- 700 014, Tel.: (033) 22273773, Telefax: 22275247 E-mail:kolkata@newagepublishers.com
- 16-A, Jopling Road, **Lucknow**-226 001. Tel.: (0522) 2209578, 4045297, Telefax: 2204098, E-mail: lucknow@newagepublishers.com
- 142C, Victor House, Ground Floor, N.M. Joshi Marg, Lower Parel, **Mumbai**- 400 013, Tel.: (022) 24927869, Telefax: 24915415 E-mail: mumbai@newagepublishers.com
- 22, Golden House, Daryaganj, **New Delhi**- 110 002. Tel.: (011) 23262370, 23262368, Telefax: 43551305, E-mail: sales@newagepublishers.com

ISBN : 978-81-224-2214-6

Rs. 150.00

C-10-06-4730

Printed in India at Ramprintograph, Delhi.
Typeset at In-house.

PUBLISHING FOR ONE WORLD
NEW AGE INTERNATIONAL (P) LIMITED, PUBLISHERS
4835/24, Ansari Road, Daryaganj, New Delhi-110002
Visit us at **www.newagepublishers.com**

With love to

Sankar, Prabha, Subramani and Lavanya.

Our beloved daughters-in-law discovered
In us another set of parents; we, in them,
Daughters that birth did not bless us with.

FOREWORD

Throughout the centuries of mankind's existence and the evolving of his industries and businesses, individuals and groups have searched diligently for ways to improve value; i.e. value of what they use and produce. During these searches, various tools have been developed, some of which have included productivity drivers, partnerships and alliances; "Just In Time", "Zero Defects" programs; Kaizen, continuous improvement projects; schemes for humanizing work, work centers; and many others too numerous to list here. Some of these have been quite successful; others have resulted in failure and the destuction of values.

The desire for and the achievement of value is basic. It is the goal of each individual to search for, plan for and work for, throughout the life cycle. However, the means of attaining the desired value is often taken for granted. Yet the methods of attaining that which is sought after is seldom taught in the educational system, industry or organization. Management of Value is not something that comes from human nature. Management of Value is something that must be learned.

Highlighting this learning need, Mr S.S. Iyer, the author, takes the reader over numerous elements that are critical to the attainment of value. Mr Iyer is quite knowledgeable, qualified and is a Certified Value Specialist (CVS). He has conducted numerous workshops to "Manage for Value." He started out with traditional Value Engineering, on engineering items and purchased materials; extended the methodology into the process industry; consolidated applications to every management and economic decision making activity. Based on his experience, he has detailed a range of ways by which the individual or group can achieve value enhancement.

The worldwide challenge is now on to develop better and better products, processes and services and at the same time lower costs. Mr. Iyer in this book has put forth for industries, institutions and universities a variety of ways to create, build and add value[1] to all products[2].

Yours for better value,
Arthur E. Mudge, CVS, Fellow
Vice President Value Planning (Retd.)
Joy Manufacturing Company
Pittsburgh, PA, USA

1. "Value" is the lowest cost to reliably accomplish the product's functions and specifications.
2. "Product" is anything which is the result of someone's labor or mental applications.

Preface to the Third Edition

From the dawn of civilisation, the goal of business and industry has been to cater to a need and earn a reward or profit from the customer or the user. He or she will continue to buy and use the item as long as it provides some value, meaning both performance and satisfaction.

All costs are for functions which satisfy needs effectively. That is why increasing emphasis is currently being placed and will continue to be placed on cost improvement all around. Managing for Values for which, value engineering was specifically created by the Late Larry Miles, both by refining the functions in the item and by cost improvement preventing unnecessary use of resources. That is the crucial need today.

I hope that this publication serves the need of all key personnel in business and industry to build their skill to mage for value, as a way of life.

S.S. Iyer

Preface to the Second Edition

After decades of prosperity, expansion and diversification, industries lost sight of "value." Today, the importance of value has become the cost of leadership, differentiation and focus. Only by examining all the sources of value in a broad and integrated way can they stay one step ahead. To enable which, as specific guidelines for developing sound strategies and for putting them into practice, I had attempted to collate experiences that enthused my humble success. In the first book, *Value Engineering - A How To Manual,* I dealt with the mechanics of making value studies in industries. In the companion book, *Managing for Value,* I took a holistic approach and extended the value adding possibilities to other unexplored facets, central to management. Together, the two books addressed most of the questions critical to make and sustain total value offerings.

The books were originally structured for combined use. However, many readers have requested that they may be made independent. In order to do so, I have, in this revision, fully described the value management process, added the basic forms for value studies and made other appropriate modifications.

I trust that this revised edition would better serve the industries, institutions and all managers, to create, build and add value in all that they do and make.

S.S. Iyer

Preface to the First Edition

Fascinated by the concept of value and its wealth creating potential, I began teaching and practicing 'Value Engineering' in mid-sixties. Now, after about four decades, I continue to be intrigued, by the spectacular benefits, that *Managing for Value* can, and can alone, endow.

In my earlier book, *Value Engineering,* I dealt with the mechanics of making value studies in industries. Implementing the findings would enable achievement of better results in hardware projects, primarily through improvements in performance capability, refinements in functions (design, manufacture and procurement) and lowering of costs. In this companion book, *Managing for Value,* I begin where *Value Engineering* left off.

The concept of value is central to all management. It is applicable to all economic decision-making. A holistic view of the entire firm and the economic environs would reveal the vast expanse of unexplored facets, central to value. Among them, important are the internal value-adding continuum, external inter-related value chains, cost effectiveness, quality affordability, and stake holder value. These are some of the value-adding possibilities covered in this book.

Each book is independent, except, where, for reasons of clarity and continuity, some overlaps and repetitions were unavoidable. Read together, the two books address most of the pressing questions, critical to make and sustain progressively superior, total value offering, in the face of challenges of advancing technology, global competition and changing economies. Doing more, better, or faster, is no way to meet these challenges. Doing different, acquiring new skills, revising the strategies, changing the logistics and implementing action, are. This book is a guide to sharpen the knowledge, hone the skills and direct creative talents, in the pursuit of this goal.

The book collates and makes available, at a single point, a vast milieu of erudite thoughts, information and data: some, gathered over years of study and observation; and many, borrowed from a variety of sources. To the sources and their architects, the savants before me, I express my deep gratitude, whether acknowledged in the text, or inadvertently overlooked.

This is a practical book. It deals with opportunities to succeed.

Having a prosperous future depends on how effectively one can reduce costs, adapt to change and build new relationships. For which, it is hoped that *Managing for Value* would become an indispensable guide for the new millennium.

Pittsburgh PA, USA **S.S. Iyer**

Contents

MANAGING FOR VALUE: AN OVERVIEW

- Value: The Core
- Lessons to Learn
- Things to Come: More of Values
- Change for Value
- Success through Value
- Practical Values
- Excellence and Value
- Improve for Value
- Value Orientation
- Customer and Value
- Innovate for Value
- Value Adders
- Business Realities
- Manage for Value

1 MANAGING FOR VALUE: AN OVERVIEW

VALUE: THE CORE

What is the world scenario today? Spectacular human progress, reflecting the contributions of knowledge and technology to society.

Knowledge is the distinct resource of any business or industry. From the start of recorded history to date, it has been growing exponentially. It is estimated that information is doubling every eighteen months. Technical knowledge is said to double itself every six to eight years. Eighty to ninety percent of the Scientists, Engineers, Technicians and Professionals who ever lived are alive today, and are endeavoring to unravel new truths. Reading is the path to knowledge. Knowledge is not only power, but also, the crux of competitive advantage. Even more so, in this technology age. Anyone can copy other's plans, products, processes and procedures. However, no one can duplicate the company's intellectual capital - knowledge and know how - the real source of **values**.

Technology is knowledge, systematically applied to useful purposes. Evolving in leaps and bounds, it will only be advancing and accelerating. The evolution and successful acceptance of technology will be directly proportional to the ability of the technology to improve the quality of human life. A firm is a collection of activities that employ technology, in some form or the other, for its performance. Technological change, shortening the average life cycle of products, leads to new products, new equipment that produce them, and new tools that assist production. It also reduces the time-distances between two points on the earth, and so, increases the speed with which one transacts business. Technology has powerful effect on cost and differentiation and pervades the value chain. It is more than robots replacing people. It is aiding people to do more with same talent and time. That is why, customers and users prefer products and services with latest technology and producers favour technological change, per se.

Expanding knowledge and advancing technology are at the core of everything: everything of value.

LESSONS TO LEARN

In the 19th century, industrial revolution demonstrated technology's power in improving human existence. In the 20th century, science, transformed into usable industrial technology, continued to hold mastery over the material world, with spectacular wealth-creating additions.

A hundred years ago, the idea of men in space, a person living with an implanted organ, or a device capable of following half a billion instructions per second, would have been considered absurd; even ridiculous. Fifty years ago, none had heard of jumbo jets, sound barrier, guided missile, re-usable spacecraft, satellite communication, color television, video cassette recorders, cellular phones, photo copiers, fax machines, answering machines, e-mail, lap-top computers, bio-genetics or bio-engineering. Global commerce and travel were limited to a few multinational companies and their employees. Macro Polo took several days to travel from Venice to China. A century later, the supersonic jet takes but hours. The telegram from the detective chasing the fictional Phileas Fogg of Jules Verne took hours to catch up with him. The transatlantic cable made conversation instantaneous and simultaneous for 130. Now, the fiber optic cable, (as inexpensive as copper wire to install), carries 500,000 messages at a time. So fast, it can transmit 10 billion bytes of information per second and at dramatically lower costs.

Years ago, the issue was to manage technology - metallurgical, chemical, engineering, electronics, nuclear, etc. It was enough to delegate it to a technical specialist. The specialist went to work and found some competitive advantage. Thus, textile technology improved spinning of cotton and weaving of textiles. Instrument technology helped better process controls. Engineering technology led to mechanisation, mass production and economies of scale.

Then, it became managing the use of technology to problems. The focus shifted to choosing a specific technology from many and using it on the jobs, to secure better business results. It involved the user. If the user knew what additions were wanted, and had the resources, these were acquired and used. Mechanisation was used to speed up production and reduce labour; automation, to produce mass at low costs; and robots, to increase manufacturing flexibility. Thus, coal, gas, oil and nuclear fission became available for power generation; and electronics, pneumatics and hydraulics, for instruments in industrial controls.

It has now become managing with technology, to search and exploit new opportunities, for satisfying human wants and needs. There are many: namely, information technology, micro technology, nano technology, biotechnology, and what have you. For example, Wal-Marts' success is in managing the use of two: computer technology and information sharing, in a creative way. Their system, hooked up to vendors' computers and scanners, made it a QR (Quick Response) shipments system. It keeps Wal-Mart shelves stocked just right, all the time, and at lowest costs. The VEC process, a digitally controlled chemical molding system, will make almost any product, anywhere, anytime; and is operable at site or remotely, via the internet.

These, we now know, are counter-productive:

1. **Line production,** in which different machines are laid out in a line along which the materials flow.
2. **Process organization,** in which materials go to several departments and sections, before completion.
3. **Functional organization of managers and office workers,** in their paper work, where several departments and sections have to manage or process the work.
4. Pursuit of **economy of scale.**
5. **Ordering in different sizes** of parts needed to make the same product.

Leading automakers are endeavouring to combine electric motors, batteries and smaller, more efficient gasoline engines into computer-controlled systems that consume less energy and emit less pollution than today's models.

Technology decisions have integrated with business decisions. Also involved is the timing for abandoning an old technology, when its limit of exploitation is imminent; and the launching of new ones. Austrian and Japanese steel makers used a technological innovation – oxygen blown converters; and US steel makers, Nucor and Lone Star – continuous casting; to create improvements within the value adding chain in the age old, traditional steel making technology.

Learning from the past, we progress into the future, escalating endeavours to discover ever more effective ways of turning knowledge and technology into commercially useful new products and services of value.

THINGS TO COME: MORE OF VALUE

Joseph A. Schumpster, the eminent economist, defined the role of modem business as "to carry out new combinations that will create new products, new methods of production, new markets, new systems of organisation," (Clifford Jr. D.K., 1985). New tools and techniques; new ways of creating, manufacturing and delivering current items; and new ways of buying, selling, distributing and communicating. New habits and attitudes, new perceived values and new everything. New will be the way of life hereafter.

To illustrate, take a single product of daily use: the razor for shaving. In its simplest form, the straight razor consisted of a sharp edged steel blade attached to a handle. Any skilled artisan could make it. It was a one-time purchase that could be sharpened and re-used a number of times. When not many users were comfortable with so dangerous a tool, in the hands of the barber and on ones neck, it evolved into the more convenient, do-it-yourself safety razor. The safety razor was in two parts: a reusable holder and a use-and-throw-away blade. To the user, cost per shave was very small. However, for the producer, it required technology, mechanised lines and special skills, to make and supply them. Then, came the variety in consumables: interchangeable blades, double edge blades, and longer lasting stainless steel blades. Another was the low cost disposable, for a single use. These were the result of advances in steel making and production technology. Each had its life, performance, price and customer value characteristics. Gillette came out with Trac II (two-bladed razor), Altra (adjustable two-bladed razor), Sensor (shock absorbent razor), Sensor excel (technically improved), and now, Mach 3 (spring mounted three-bladed razor) that gently sets up your beard for the closest shave. One after the other. Within a period of 15 years. The razor of value was, each time, new: a different modification, an innovation, or a concept.

Proctor and Gamble introduced the first laundry detergent, Tide, in 1946. In 1984, it added unscented Tide and Liquid Tide; in 1988, Tide with bleach; in 1990, Concentrated Ultra Tide; and in 1992, Tide with Bleach alternative. In a single year, 1991, sixty-four new varieties of spaghetti sauce appeared in the market. In 1992 alone, Heinz introduced more than 500 new products, worldwide. Rubbermaid turns out an average of one new product a day; and Gillette, 20 annually.

Forecasters predict a future of technological opportunities in space, time and mass, far more sweeping than what has ever happened. Some of the emerging technologies that would sweep us into the 21st century are powerful computers, intelligent software, smart manufacturing systems and multifunction office devices tied to a ubiquitous communications network.

In the offing are new ways of getting things done: in manufacturing, communicating, delivery channels and more. Does not the cost of flying between cities on a major air line decline to almost half of the cost of travel by Grey Hound buses ? Production is estimated to go up three- or four-fold. It would become progressively more automated, skill-intensive and decentralised. Information would become inexpensive, universal and instantaneously accessible, on demand. Strong and fast growth in the consumer markets would be on consumer "desires," rather than "needs." In the industrial markets, it would be on "urgencies of competition," "lowering of costs," and "improving performance." More and more goods and services would be evaluated, selected, and ordered from homes. More and more operations would be air borne, on line and real time.

It has been predicted that, in the years ahead, the undermentioned items will grow strong and fast: wine and spirits; electronic equipment, both at home and at work: telephone and office equipment; leisure activities, like hobbies, collecting, reading, music making; health and beauty; gifts; eating out; cruises, tours, etc.

The trend is seen everywhere. In ways to treat diseases before they occur. In superior, high performance materials, (light alloys, new composites, plastics and ceramics), for use in computers and communications. In compact, long lasting and highly portable energy sources. In miniaturised electronic equipment, for personal use. In building almost all man-made objects a thousand times smaller than what micro-technology did. In cost effective systems, that integrates power, sensors and controls. In hybrid fuel vehicles, reusable space vehicles and miles-wide satellites in space. In educational games and computerised simulations. In capacity to mold and simulate just about anything.

It would revolutionise our life styles and work styles. Our hearing, vision and response mechanisms are already getting sharper, to be of value, in tune with our environment. Our brains would soon have the capability for simultaneous processing of multiple data, from multiple sources of information. Workplace is becoming virtual - anywhere, anytime. There would be no "jobs;" but only work - seamless, as it moves between home, office, telecommunication centers, on the road, or at the locations of suppliers, contractors, and strategic partnering allies; as well as endless, as it rolls through a 24-hour day. Neither would it be a "specified or defined or prescribed task." Nor laid out by some organisation, which one performs and gets paid for. The criterion for work would be the value that it adds.

Every person would have to constantly re-shape and recall his strengths and skills and re-negotiate his or her value for the organisation that is paying.

CHANGE FOR VALUE

As we move into the new millennium, we are entering an era of constant change. Becoming - and remaining - the winner, will require an ever increasing ability to make the right decisions and to execute those decisions more effectively than the competitors. Success arises from being different. And, then being prepared to change again. To quote Charles Darwin, "to search and exploit new opportunities, for satisfying human wants and needs."

Too much is changing for anyone to be complacent about value. We live in an ever-changing world. Things have changed in the past. It will continue to change in the future also. There is always something in the horizon that forces change. Change and survival go hand in hand. Again, Darwin's law of survival of the fittest governs the survival of products, services and societies: those most responsive to change. Value is the force that determines what will survive, grow and prosper.

Change is disturbing and difficult. Dinosaurs died off because the species was unable to adapt fast enough to changing conditions, warns Prof. C. K. Prahalad. The older and larger the firm, the more difficult it will be to change. Worse, if the firm, successful in the past, views what worked would work equally well in the coming years. The French philosopher Voltaire cautioned, "if you are doing anything today in the same way you did it a year ago, you are probably doing it wrong." What he said 200 years ago is especially applicable now. Technology, globalisation and the demand for customisation, enhancements, speed and cost containment are driving change.

The importance of developing a good strategy responsive to change cannot be over emphasised. It is crucial that the change should bring in improvement. To change and to improve are two different things. It requires thorough understanding of the new direction, willingness to change and purposeful execution.

Changing the skill base of the firm is both difficult and time-consuming. Obviously, it involves training for the needed skills. More importantly, it also involves unlearning the old skills and rehabilitating those who are not trainable. People, who, for years, used hammer and tongs, will not easily transform into machinists of computer integrated manufacturing systems. Neither the Manager, so far comfortable with carrying on, will willingly disturb the status quo ante. Change of any kind is a war against old habits, biased thinking and personal stake. It is a struggle with fear, anger and uncertainty.

Change is the key to progress. To quote Charles Kittering, the famous inventor, "the world hates change, but it is the only thing that brings progress." The challenge of each century, and so, for the 21st Century, is going to be change: change in products and services, change in technologies, change in national and international trade, change of every kind, every day. The phenomenon of change is just not limited to any one area. The tactics for coping with change are three. Ignore it and let it happen. Anticipate it and adapt it. Create change and profit from it.

For example. For generations past, Insurance companies, Drug makers and similar others settle customer claims "out of court," as the less cost and less embarrassing means of dealing with this inevitable menace, basing their policy on "Business decisions." This has led to consumers taking undue advantage, unfairly targeting big and rich companies, for even trivial things. Wal-Mart, the retail giant, is trying to change this. Wal- Mart is now settling claims, using a policy of "Legal decisions." It accepts claims for which it is liable, and fights others that lack merit. Other companies are watching the outcome, to join in.

Good management works miracles. However, mediocre management is the norm. That is because capable management is so extraordinarily difficult. Demands on the manager are so wide and so great that they are nearly impossible to meet. The Manager has to acquire all the traditional management skills: like finance, cost control, resource allocation, product development, marketing, etc. The Manager has also to master the management arts: like writing, speaking, strategy, negotiation; appraisal, ethics, clairvoyance, etc. Besides, the Manager has to demonstrate the qualities of leadership and integrity; and play the roles of friend, mentor and coach. The Manager today must be educated, trained and developed in what nobody knew yesterday; and prepared for what must be known tomorrow; and build expertise for what one knows not yet. The Manager has to become a jack of all tools, techniques, functions and strategies and master of every one of them: a value adder. This is only the beginning. The successful Manager of the future will be a change agent, creating change for a purpose: *values.*

How organisations create change (how big and how fast); and how they manage change (how it exploits every opportunity to create value); will make the difference between sweet success and bitter failure.

SUCCESS THROUGH VALUE

Success once depended on access to material. For example, a steel plant owned captive ore and coal deposits and stone quarries. Vertical integration meant uninterrupted production. Success also depended on size, like the super large plants, biggest machines, longest production runs, or most market share. It may not enable making the best product (or service). However, it could make the most at lowest costs. Cost was invariably a dominant consideration. Success also came from strategies, like making everything within the company. It controlled availability and quality. Being the sole possessor of critical product knowledge, patents and copyrights, meant monopoly: again success.

Where it used to be the product that let the companies win, it has now become the capability to create it quicker. Consider these. The steam engine, was conceived in 1680 (Denis Papin). It was built to do useful work in 1712 (Thomas Newcomen). It pulled the first train on a commercial railroad in 1830 (Rocket of George Stephenson). It took another 50 years to become efficient and 20 more, to go into worldwide use. The diesel engine designed in 1897 became the means of propulsion in 1935. In contrast, the microchip, developed in the early 1970s, became the essential element for computers in 10 years, and globally available in another ten. The twelfth century invention, gun powder, took 200 years to be applied in warfare; whereas, atomic fission, discovered in 1939, was made into the atom bomb within 5 years. Similarly, it took 37 years for the radio to become popular; Web took only 4 years to reach the homes. Blue-collar jobs were sophisticated in 100 years, but the white-collar regime got installed in ten. Blue-collar robots took jobs out of the factory, warehouse and dockside. May be, white-collar robots would take off 95 percent of the drudgery. Certainly, all things are now evolving towards better and fitter states.

Success came from strengths in machines, the quick producer, replacing workers. The factory system views labour as a tool, for either specialisation or elimination with labour saving devices. Mechanisation, automation and robots became reliable replacements for humans. At first, the blue-collar jobs vanished. Then, accounting and finance jobs, taken over by batch-processing computers. Computers are replacing now white-collar workers, seeping into the ranks of middle management.

It appears as though there is no limit to replacing humans in the workplace. For, technological advances in electronically controlled machines are getting smarter and better. It would have made matters worse had not the single-handed, problem-solving specialist started giving way to extensive team approaches. The worker is coming back now as the primary means of adding value to product, process and service.

Success stems from knowledgeably applying a combination of available resources to the needs of each individual situation. Clinging to yesterday's methods of manufacture and product lines, tools, techniques, mindsets and attitudes is a prescription for suicide. Former assumptions, practices and procedures, methods and strategies are increasingly changing. Even what the industrial leaders think as the work their companies should do. This implies that individuals have to increasingly and continuously learn and relearn value adding knowledge and skills.

To be successful, industries would have to create and maintain relevant and distinct product (or service) capabilities and features. Besides, they would have to meet continuously and continually, all the growing needs of the customer, with cost-effective, quality products and services that give them profitable advantage. At the same time, they would also have to respect and safeguard the interests of all the stakeholders. They have to do everything short of reinventing their companies.

They would have to assimilate the scientific discoveries, technologies, inventions and innovations, in such a way that practical values flow to the user and the customer, in the most orderly and economical way.

PRACTICAL VALUES

Industry's business of making things remains the bulwark of the economic system and the nation's standard of living. Manufacturing in conjunction with extractive industries and agriculture - creates the real wealth.

Industries are right now riding the crest of a tidal wave of change. The industrial age brought us products such as heavy machinery, farm equipment and home appliances - things that could be touched, seen and demonstrated. The mass production model was the foundation upon which industries grew and succeeded. Mass has ceased to be the key. Value, measured in customers' terms, is. That is, *making and supplying a product or service, of better relative customer-perceived value.*

The cornerstone of producing anything in volume is standardisation: and it eliminates choice. Now, product choices are exploding exponentially: in makes, types, sizes, shapes, features, brand names, and country of origin. Thus, mass production is giving way to the new economic model of *mass customisation.* A great variety of products are made at mass production prices, using common platforms and adding customising options in the final stages of production. Mass marketing has changed to *pin point marketing of a unique product or service.*

The information age that followed the industrial age brought intangibles. Examples are resources that involve intellect and the ability to gather, analyse, transmit and synthesise information: computers, media and print on paper that makes information resource universal, and accessible to every user. The competitive edge has shifted from managing physical resources towards strategic *utilisation of the business information, technology and people, to create value for the customers.*

To gain a jump on the competitors that cannot be readily matched, change is imperative. Even changing the rules as Dell Computers did. Dell, so small to compete with others, broke the rule of show-casing computers in stores and went in for mail order and direct sales, to grow to a $ 800 million company in five years. If one does not change the rules oneself, advancing technology will change them. Just as the Japanese did, revolutionising the consumer electronics industry by pushing a product - the video cassette recorder - that an American company, Ampex, invented, but dismissed as a toy for the rich. Even, change established practices.

Organizations are loath to admit problem. While touting commitment to customer satisfaction and customer delight.

As the world becomes more global, it is helpful to understand what values, if any, are universal, which is the basic building block of value-based leadership.

In a rapidly changing world, values are the only stabilizing factor delight, they falter in customer relationships.

When an individual is not performing, the immediate reaction is to look for a scape goat. Honesty yields to *palatable truths.* Honesty would mean doing what you are preparing to do; thinking before judging; avoiding any finger pointing; owning up weaknesses and mistakes; etc. Honesty fosters a sense of personal accountability, enabling quicker responses to internal and external changes. Voicing problems, owning them and fixing them improves the chances of success.

The compulsion for industries is not only to exist, survive and compete; but, to grow. Growth is the result of success; of offering what the customers want, buy and pay for; of using economic resources effectively and making profits needed for expansions. Growth is not a matter of simple expansion or addition of facilities. Physical increase in output per capita would mean re-designing of methods and equipment. Growth also does not come from mergers, acquisitions or diversification. On an average, mergers decrease efficiency. Many conglomerates, built on false synergy, failed. Gillette, which added Parker, Paper Mate and Waterman to its line of business (7.5 percent), found the hard way that people buying personal hygiene products do not think of pens and stationary items on the same shopping trip. Many unrelated acquisitions were divested (ITT) just as in this case. Diversification into areas where a company lacked knowledge, skill and core competency proved disastrous. Growth is the by-product of doing many things right and resolving many complexities. Especially with "product diversity, volume, technology and systems relationships; numbers, types and geography of distribution channels and end consumers; and growing pressures in external environment - government, labour, competition, world economy and society in general," (Clifford, D.K., 1985). Wal-Mart exemplifies this. It started out in 1945 as a Five and Dime variety store, offering friendly service and lowest prices to rural Americans. Great was its commitment that it persevered with missionary zeal. It turned into a discount business by 1960. Now, it is in the third position in retailing in all USA. It is vying to supersede Sears and K. Mart with the next generation Hyper-Mart and Super Center.

The company of the future will be the one that views its business creatively and from the customers' perspective.

It will garner and adapt need-based opportunities to grow and prosper. It will create competitive advantage by finding the right products and services to offer, and doing things better, faster and different. The US railroads considered their job as laying tracks and connecting places. They missed profiting from new technologies and seeing the business, creatively: transporting people and goods. The Postal services viewed its job as moving mail and Federal Express saw it as satisfying each customer with overnight delivery. The focus of starbuck is on building one of the world's most recognized consumer brands, instead of simply opening more stores.

EXCELLENCE AND VALUE

Excellence is not an art, but a habit. Continuous and profitable growth comes from excellence. To quote Tata's Chairman, late J.R.D. Tata, "always aim at perfection, for only then will you achieve excellence," (Lala, 1981). The journey towards excellence is a never-ending road. Something, that is never completed but always striven for, excellence is a multi-dimensional concept that encompasses hard technologies, soft, people management issues, and scores of other things. Excellence is to do a common thing in an uncommon way, says Brooker T. Washington. "*Excellence is surpassing customer expectations* at a price that represents value to them and delivering consistent performance without repair or excuse" (Harrington, James H., 1987). Improving the excellence of everything we do would raise productivity, eliminate waste, and enable providing customers with world class products and services. That is basic. Only excellence earns a profit.

Top performance, i.e., *excellence, is required of every one to sustain progressive improvement.*

IMPROVE FOR VALUE

Intellectual property of the firm is based on ideas and concepts – not machinery and processes. People are the greatest assets. They have to be valued above everything else. Human capital is the collective skills and knowledge of the firm's workforce. That is what creates value. Enhancing the value of the people means enhancing the value of the firm. When people feel valued, they would work extra hours willingly. When they do not feel valued, they would still work, but reluctantly and with resentment. Firms will attract employees who are a reflection of the corporate values. Talent will migrate to companies that value people. How the firm adds value to their people will determine how they contribute and what they contribute to add value to the firm. Therefore, giving people a clear understanding of how their jobs fit within the firm's value chain is the biggest motivator.

To stay in business, one must continue to improve, enhance current product or service, and develop variations and incremental improvements that can make all the difference in style, shape, quality, cost and sales appeal. However, organisations make only routine searches to improve. The common tendency is to reach for the latest tool or technique and apply it. Since these are additions superimposed on the top of existing capabilities, the net gains are often incremental. Then it becomes a quest for a superior tool or technique for the next trial, some months later. The cycle perpetuates itself. The rapid pace of changes, worldwide, puts progressively increasing pressure on organisations to try even harder to improve every thing they do.

Improvement does not just happen. Neither does it come from one major change. All technical, engineering and equipment changes have limitations in terms of productivity improvements. Similarly, products reach a limit of their improvement possibilities. Besides, not all product improvements are of value. Fortunately, when all the people are involved with their hearts and minds, the improvements could become unlimited. Improvements are the result of desire and pursuit. It is pursued by organising for it: like responsive product development, maintaining manufacturing excellence, permanently correcting many small problems and ensuring that they do not repeat themselves, innovation, etc. Studies show that it requires integration of nine important attributes: commitment, creativity, communication, mind set for service, flexibility, speed, partnership, trust and freedom from fear.

There have been many approaches to secure improvements. Traditional improvement efforts are *ad hoc,* usually initiated only when a major recurring problem is identified. Then, the approach is re-active, instead of pro-active. Further, the efforts usually taper off with time or with incremental gains. Incremental improvements are only temporary relief or a feeling of renewed competitiveness, cautions the Re-engineering advocate. "If you go for a 10 percent improvement, you only get better sameness," (James Champy, 1995). Incremental improvement assumes that the company has time to make the change. Also, that the organisation would self-correct. General Motors and Commerce Clearing House (a speciality publisher), were lulled into complacency with incremental changes - and, near collapse. *Evolutionary improvement,* not incremental; big and fast; *continuous and continual:* those are the imperatives to excel. Each time making some improvements to current product (or service) and coming a little closer to the needs of the customer. To be the leader in any industry or business, one has to constantly find ways to do things better, faster and different. "In an average year, Sony introduces 1,000 new or updated products or 4 per working day," (Schlender, B.R., 1992), and a new Walkman model every 3 weeks.

To improve, the conventional thrust has been, and will continue to be, on production, productivity, yields and efficiencies. That is because the industries are designed for economies of scale, specialisation in work, and fixing what needs fixed. Breaking work down into tasks, assigning them to experts, simplifying work flows and creating assembly groups, add more departments and units; but no value to the product or the company. Even performance-, efficiency-, incentive-, and motivation-oriented approaches are superimposed on already attained positions of strength, yielding diminishing returns. Task force focused on internally generated measures and past data, weeding out unnecessary activities and restructuring management layers help only in catching up; and not exploiting new advantages or opportunities. Important tasks, no doubt; but, though previously good enough, no longer adequate.

We need something more, a value orientation.

The old idea of success was to build an enduring, great company (like IBM). But, even they maintain superior returns only for a limited time, often less than one decade. McKinsey & Company, the blue chip consulting firm, argues that, in times of rampant and uncertain change, as at present, it will be better for the company to improve continuously. They advocate that the company should turn its back on profitable products and pour resources into unproven, but promising technologies. They urge that it constantly reassesses its business and remains alert to the unknown possibilities. They feel that destruction is difficult to master. For that matter, even innovation. They feel that only surprise earns extraordinary returns. Finding familiar facts comforting and explaining away inconsistencies is no way.

VALUE ORIENTATION

Manufacturing adds value to the raw material and creates wealth. To maximise, the key was to use slick production techniques, matching technical leads, and making painstaking improvements. It is a time- and quality-sensitive activity, linked to several areas, both within the company and outside the company. Time is another component of value. Time compression and flexibility are prerequisites for being more responsive to the customers. Then the goal becomes optimisation for the entire enterprise, rather than tasks, which only maximises output. In the lead is programmable automation or Flexible Manufacturing System (FMS). FMS can turn out a wide range of products on the same line, shifting instantly from one model to the next. With FMS, it is claimed that the efficiency of both capital and labour can be doubled (or even trebled) and defects, reduced considerably. It can also reduce the time it takes to introduce new products by as much as 90 per cent. Customer relationship becomes impervious to competition. The idea of Agile Manufacturing is to make a profit on a volume of one. That is what the Pittsburgh Steel Stamping plant of General Motors, built in 1950, is trying to convert to. Such advances notwithstanding, manufacturing will remain a very small component of the entire *value-delivering-continuum* - that begins with Research and Development, progresses through Product Design and Manufacturing and After Sales Service and extends to Suppliers, Distributors and Customers.

Every one in every function must become fully involved and committed members of the value adding team.

As the tidal wave of technology gathers force and crashes upon us, we will work more efficiently. Just as mechanisation did at the turn of the century, automation, robots and electronics are changing the way we create and manufacture products. As evidence are the transistor, (invented in 1928), the telephones, (in wide spread use since 1940) and the telephone-cum-television information services. Televisions are evolving into computers. Computers are turning into video games, the next generation super-power, video game players. Soon to come are the new breed of gizmos that fall somewhere in between, from satellite driven global positioning devices for cars to cellular pagers that beam messages directly into your wristwatches. Technological advances are fast raising *efficiencies;* but, the question is will they add *effectiveness,* which combination is of real value ?

Doing better anything being done begets efficiency. Increasing efficiency is a minimum condition for survival after achieving success. Early efforts focused primarily on efficiency improvements. Increasing profits through internal efficiency has limitations. Yet, efficiency is the call, without regard for long term consequences. What appears to be efficiency may actually result in inefficiency. In the obsession with efficiency and the zeal to become more and more efficient at things, value is lost. To be inefficient is bad; to be efficient is good. However, not at the cost of values. For instance, using new technologies, appliances are becoming more efficient. Yet energy use has not come down. Interconnected grids have rendered whole sections of the country vulnerable to loss of power. Medicine is identifying illnesses more and more efficiently, but the conditions seem abnormal. Cost of health care escalates upward, with little benefit. Positive screening tests enable doctors to treat illness efficiently and well. That is, even if the survivor wishes to get transferred to another doctor. The patients do not live long enough for their illness to become life threatening. Demands of efficiency made Air lines to work to the hub and spoke system, but it takes travelers often in the wrong direction, to get to their destinations. Voice mail may be more efficient from the business perspective, but it ended the receptionist's job. The filling stations became more efficient when they transferred all services to the customer. Now the supermarket is following suit asking people to learn how to check out. Indeed, every aspect of life is being dominated by the demands of efficiency. Therefore, who knows it would spread to the better qualities of life, conveniences and things that count: *values.*

The need today is for effectiveness. Such as: performance effectiveness, like numbers per day, tons per acre, miles per gallon, etc.; yield effectiveness, like pounds of product per pound of raw material; cost effectiveness, like quality per cost, reliability per cost; customising; timeliness; service; guarantee; etc. Today's efforts focus more on effectiveness–doing things right. Effectiveness deals with sustaining a strategy; efficiency, with the present utilisation of resources. Effectiveness is more than efficiency, or aims, or outputs, or minimum costs, although it includes all of these. "Efficiency is concerned with doing things right. Effectiveness is doing the right things," (Drucker, P., 1975). If we can get people to focus on doing the right things and doing them right, we will have accomplished all. The million-dollar question is, how. Challenging efficiency is easier if it were possible to prioritize and discriminate between various items on the basis of value.

CUSTOMER AND VALUE

This is the age of customisation. Gone are the days of producing what you want to make or what you want to sell. It was conventionally Market Research, who surveyed what the customer wants and who defined what the customer trends are. Delegating away this important job of figuring out the customers' needs, it often was a surprise, if the product turned out to be what the customer really wanted. If not, the product underwent modifications and redevelopment, many times over. Even with all that, customer requirements were seldom fully met.

Today, it is the customer, who says what is wanted or needed; and the manufacturer makes it. The onus is on the manufacturer to increase the value of their offerings and cozy up to the customer on his own terms. In the mid-century, when everything was big, (roomy, luxurious automobiles), they wanted it small (compacts). The manufacturers ushered in the micro age. The transistor, integrated circuits, batteries, computer chips, digital watches, calculators, were in the lead of miniaturisation. Now, they desire more power: like four-wheel drive, which the automobile makers are now adding as standard in a variety of cars. They desire more features: like multi channels that TV makers are adding to their wares and computer makers to memory in PCs. They ask even more frills: such as form fitting seats, solar tint glass, remote locking system, in autos; and mini works of art in CD covers. In treatment of emergencies, people are becoming less tolerant of delays or mistakes. Medi-Cam and EMX Cards, recently developed, allow doctor and medics in the field to communicate via satellite, virtually anywhere in the world and access to database for the individual's medical history. The day is not far off when the doctor will consult the genetic profile recorded on a chip to design a prescription just for a specific person.

With competition being what it is, the customers today have more options from which to choose. In the past, adequate quality and affordable price were good enough to attract and keep customers. Not so anymore. People, by nature, are never satisfied. The power of the customer is growing exponentially. They increasingly want a broad assortment of incentives. Consumer tastes are not only changing, but, often even becoming unpredictable. They do not know what cannot they demand, need or want, unless and until they see it. When they see it, they want more of the things they value. Value is what they get out of the product or service. If they value quality, performance or life, they want it higher. If they value convenience, they want it even easier and faster. If they value service, they want it more promptly, on demand. If they value low cost, they want it lower still. Mass production met only the basic criteria of consumption–affordability. Like what Cannon did in cameras. The German champions were comprehensively beaten by the use of mass production methods, to offer high precision 35 mm single lens reflector photography to the market.

Once the customers find the product affordable, they ante their demands on every front besides price: quality, service, features, novelty, timeliness, guarantees, etc. When these needs are met, they want satisfaction. They look for individually designed products, services and communications, matched to their individual tastes. They want also to be pleased about their purchase decision, pampered and gratified. Further, should the product fail, they want compensation.

Consumers' increasing awareness of the relationship between design, quality, price and delivery has led them to have a greater appreciation of value. They research all attributes, shop more strategically: using coupons, marketing flyers of sales and remaining loyally to price; and work hard to get the best value for their money from everything. They are not afraid to bargain their way to a better deal. They look for value-added items: like extra benefits and bottom line capabilities, quality consistency, extended warranties, quick delivery, hassle-free service, etc. Their goal is to have a customised product that is unique for them and tailored exactly for what they want it to be, and at the lowest price. They know that planning, organization and patience would be the key to savings.

It is impossible to be good at everything. Trying to be all things to all people is both complicated and wasteful. The key to failure is trying to please everybody. Xerox tried to become the provider of the office of the future. It tried to offer an integrated system of copiers to computers and everything in between. Twenty years and many billion dollars later, it still sells copiers. Nike is trying to become a sports mega supplier - everything from head to foot for the athlete. It is in the doldrums. The future belongs to the company that concentrates on what it can do best. The focus should be on what can be. It is more productive.

The more things one tries to become, the more difficult it becomes to differentiate. Companies are now differentiating themselves by concentrating all talents and faculties on one achievement - *excelling in their core capabilities.* In addition, they are honing their capabilities in one or more other components of value sought by the customers. That becomes their value offering. Westinghouse retained and expanded its broadcasting business and became CBS Corporation. It shed its power generation and defense lines. Eastman Kodak is jettisoning the legacies of failed diversification efforts and embarking on a series of digital photography initiatives. Gillette is shedding its pen and stationary line and concentrating on personal health care products.

One of the most critical moves in business today is to achieve just-in-time marketing in addition to just-in-time manufacturing - when the customer wants it, the way the customer wants it, with the quality, features and the price the customer wants. For example, in Japan, one can go to a bicycle shop, pick out the components, be measured for size, and ride out on the bicycle fitted to individual preferences and anatomies, in just one hour. The choice range: 11, 231, 862 variations of 18 bicycle models, 19 colours and parts. The Textile Clothing Technology Corporation makes T-shirts, designed by the customer, while the customer waits. Pearle Vision and Lens Crafters Inc., make custom-made eyeglasses in about an hour.

Traditional organisations were essentially marketing-driven, finance-driven, and manufacturing-driven. This is changing. Performance driven and market based solutions are steering companies into a customer-driven world. Customers have certain expectations from the product or service they buy-what it will do, convey, and so on. This is *the expected product* or service. Catering effectively to the expectations gains customer satisfaction. For instance, Boeing designs 747 features and interiors that each purchasing Airline wants.

A step forward, beyond customer satisfaction, to offer the customer more than what they can get for the current outlay, or something different, is where creativity pays. Quick chill cans, gasolene saving tires, plain paper copiers, instant photography, home banking, no wash diapers, slow release pills and so on, succeeded, because these provided creative additions that the customers never had before.

Building and offering products and services that exceed customers' expectations is *the augmented product.* Like, when VISA and Master Card issuers linked their cards to airline mileage programs, they added significant perceived value to their cards, with little change in price. When L.L. Bean introduced leather uppers and rubber lowers in their boots, it gave customers both the comfort of leather and the waterproof quality of rubber. These augmented products won *customer delight.*

Yet, another step forward is to create *raving customers.* Nordstorm, the clothier, has a matchless level of service to the customers that makes doing business with them "an experience of a life time." The Company remembers the customer's name, measurements and birthdays. That is exemplary relationship management for a retailer. Barnes and Noble Book Stores provide chairs and tables, maintain a coffee and pastry section, stay open 9 am to 11 pm, seven days in a week and schedule talk by authors and other presentations, becoming a community centre.

The progression from customer satisfaction has not ended. Now, they are creating *partnerships* with the users. For example, traditionally, in the utility business, the company's objective is to provide low cost electricity, delivered up to the meter in the user's building. Going a long way forward, they now assist the customers in meeting their every day energy needs-helping them use electricity in the way it provides the most value to them. Edison in Los Angeles is outstanding example, zealously helping customers achieve energy efficiencies and effectiveness, saving electricity, rather than burning it. That is value in use, or applied value: how much does the product or service, its quality and technology, and support services add to the customers' advantages.

Companies capable of mass customisation optimise the relationship with the customer. They close the gap between producers and customers. They involve customers right at the design stage, so that better specifications are drawn up for products to cater more effectively to customer needs. They use feed back from customers, to even develop the process of manufacture. Customers, looking for more than functional benefits-psychological and emotional - have made design economy critical.

Partnerships with suppliers and distributors optimise quality and reliability of inputs and deliveries; provide access for markets; etc. Such alliances look for complementary skill sets. Partners are treated like divisions of the same company, and as peers. Integrated, total enterprise optimisation means efficiency combined with effectiveness, and internal as well as outside focus.

Winning customers is more than a matter of providing superior quality and service. *The customers now want ever-better quality, ever-quicker response, ever-greater flexibility, and ever-greater fail-safe and ever-larger returns: or, in one word, ever-higher values.* The product or service must take the customer beyond mere satisfaction to true enthusiasm: superior customer value.

INNOVATE FOR VALUE

Economists see innovation as "changing the value and satisfaction obtained from resources by the customers." For managers, innovation "creates new and different values and new and different satisfactions, to convert a material into a resource or to combine existing resources in a new and more productive configuration" (Drucker, P., 1985). Central to innovation is value, which governs the creation, acceptance and diffusion of innovation. The straight path to quality, customer delight, competitive advantage, and so, value, would be innovation. In fact, business has only one basic function - innovation. All winning companies innovate continuously.

Innovation comes from unleashing people's power, cross-fertilisation and sharing of ideas. Innovation flourishes in working situations where employees are not afraid to fail. Innovations may be task-focussed to provide a customers' need; perfect a process that already exists; replace a link that is weak; redesign an existing old process; supply a missing link; etc. It involves focusing resources by concentrating on bringing technology to market; creating customer pull on technology; new product introduction; their quick development; reduction of time to market; increasing value returns to customers, employees and stock holders; and such like.

The customer needs are often the mother of innovation. About 70 percent of all major innovations are driven by market trend. For example, in the detergent battles of 1950, all producers were vying to make a product that would produce the "cleanest" clothes. When any detergent removed dirt, the cleaned clothes acquired a gray, dingy look. That (gray, dingy look), the consumer thought, was remnants of dirt that persisted. Whereas, in fact, it was torn and frayed fibers. The desire to have cleaner, brighter clothes was dominant with the customers. Proctor and Gamble tried and succeeded to add optical brighteners to the detergent, which reflected light, made clothes appear brighter, and so, cleaner. The consumer loved it. Tide became a roaring success. Another example is the GE Transportation Systems. They consulted in 1992 railroad executives, engineers and operators to determine the commercial and technical drivers for locomotives through 1998 and conceived a cascading multi-generation product plan to add new features. The innovations were electronic fuel injection systems, converter systems and controls added to each model through 1998. Yet another product developed on the basis of customer feedback is Word Perfect software.

Nearly half of all innovations are made from ideas initiated by customers, either guiding, or adding in some way or another, to a producer's ideas of innovation. Yet, a company cannot depend only on the customer, to tell specifically what he or she wants. Often, the customer does not know what exactly they want. No one asked for a cellular telephone, ATMs, CD player, microwave oven, or fax machine. Neither cellophane, nylon, orlon, teflon, lycron and kevlar. The customers are very adaptive in getting around the problems of the product or service. Innovative companies seek to understand world trends, regardless of their association with the present product or technology mix. They draw from these trends imaginative understanding of user needs: both expressed, as well as unarticulated (pocket size, on time delivery, untethered communication, benefit of choice, availability, speed, etc.). Jotters are made with built-in LCD watches, giving the customer the combined benefits. It requires quite a leap of imagination to empathise with human needs. Empathy to see what the customer might want, or might be made to want, in the future; to generate product or service improvements or innovations, and to provide superior value, at every point. Casio and Rubbermaid demonstrate this characteristic the best. Casio first introduced a digital watch with a built-in small calculator. Then, it put out two versions that carried respectively 50 and 100 telephone numbers in its memory. Still later, Casio added the version with world time. Rubbermaid designs innovative solutions to everyday problems in containers: Sipp'n Sport drink bottles, Lid access tool boxes, easier opening food containers for an aging population with less manual dexterity, etc.

Innovation also comes from cannibalising the products, as L'Oreal did, for its anti-wrinkle cream; or, as Mazda did, for the sports model, Miata.

Systematic analysis of demographics and other trends have opened out possibilities of innovative speciality niches. So also, powerful blending of trend analysis with core competency, and focusing in the direction of change and progress. For Sony Corporation, miniaturisation was a core competency, developed since the time of its first transistor radio, "TR-55," in the early 1950s. It was the beginning of a product line so small that they fit in a pocket. The company shrunk videotape recorders from huge machines run on vacuum tubes into compact, transistorised models. Now, it is the turn of their Walkman, Camcorder and hand held devices of all kinds. Battery makers have followed their lead. Vistakon created Acuvue, the first disposable contact lens around its manufacturing competency - lens making. Nike, found customers first and then designed and made the products just for them. Seeing that skate boarders drag their feet to brake and turn, the specialised Nike sneakers were made with extra layers of leather, double stitching, more rubber insole, etc. Thus began the Nike athletic shoe range - basket ball shoes; running shoes; walking shoes; aerobic shoes; skate board shoes; snow boarding shoes; biking shoes; et al.

While making trend analysis, one should guard against the tendency to be comforted by familiar facts and explaining away the inconsistencies. The temptation to follow trends and fashion is often overpowering. Remember in our search for the new, we sometimes re-invent the old.

Innovative companies search the whole universe for ideas to innovate. When Southwest Airlines wanted to improve turn round of its planes at airports, they studied not only what other Airlines were doing. They also watched what the pit crews at the Auto Races did to fuel and service the racing cars: similar functions at much faster speeds. They cut their turn round time by half. Granite Rock looked at operation of Automatic Teller Machines in Banks, to reduce paper work delays in their general loading operations. Toyota researchers observed how the customers loaded their groceries into the trunk of their cars, in large parking lots of Super Markets, before redesigning the trunk to provide more room and ease for sliding of packages.

There is no question but that companies should develop a systematic process of rapid innovation. For the past decade, at least, the Holy Grail of industries has been innovation. Innovation tops agendas and budgets for staff. Bulk of Hewlett Packard's revenues is derived from products less than a year old. Innovation is risky whereas, non-innovation will be fatal. Failure to innovate will mean failure to develop and focus core competency in the direction of change and progress. Remaining firmly anchored in tradition would be good for continuity, but it could lead to stagnation. It needs flexibility to adjust quickly to changing markets. Once fallen behind in the pace of innovation, it will be impossible to catch up and recover position - not just in the products, but in whole crucial technology. It needs the company's best performers. Innovation needs a greed for new things; foresight to come up with some thing totally different; unconventional thinking; and thinking without boundaries. It needs the courage to make obsolete own products and services before the competitor.

Innovation means monitoring seven sources:

Within the organisation:

(i) the unexpected

(Microwave idea came from candy melting in pocket, while standing in front of a radar magnetron),

(ii) the incongruity

(Dying shipping companies were saved by changing loads to containers),

(iii) a process need

(Preservation of enzyme made cataract operations easier), and

(iv) a sudden change

(Ford's Edsel flopped with change in lifestyle of prospective car buyers).

Outside the organisation:

(v) demographics,

(vi) change in perception, mood or meaning, and

(vii) new knowledge.

Innovation is likened to a machine. All companies have employees brimming with ideas. The problem is in culling the good ideas and making them work. Therefore, like machines, they have to be designed, oiled, powered and managed. Innovation is also likened to a garden. The germ of the ideas need germination. Therefore, the company must create conditions under which it can flourish. It takes time.

Knowledge-based innovation has the largest lead-time between investment and profitability. Those based on an analysis of unexpected successes or failures have short lead times. Potential value added improves with multiple skilled contributors.

Over the past few decades, advances in management sciences have chiefly come from efforts of organizations to systematically drive out variability and waste; and emphasise consistency. But the essense of innovation is variability and adventure.

There may be no single road to innovation; but, there are signs that you are headed in the right direction when you get to the market quicker, optimize resources and achieve globalization.

Here is list of what you can do to innovate.

- Cut product range.
- Cut variants rationalizing designs.
- Exploit cost linkages within the value chain.
- Find key parameters that the customer will focus on to make his buying decision. Use the data appropriately.
- Find how the key buying functions relate to technical performance factors and design factors for each alternative that you have. Use them to correct.
- Invent new products, re-invent own jobs and skills.
- Do simple things superbly.

VALUE ADDERS

Every company that is worth anything today, derived it from the efforts, knowledge and ingenuity of its employees. According to the book "Funky

Business," the only unique asset companies have is the brainpower of their employees. In the past, in the search for productivity, it was concentration on a plethora of tools and techniques to help employees to work faster. Now, it is a search for creativity and incentives to *help employees to become more creative.* Most major innovations come from some "crazy people" in the organisation, who have an idea for something that will work and add value. Like, the stick it notes, quick chill cans, gas saving tires, plain paper copier, instant photography, no-wash diapers, home banking, etc.

To quote Theodre Levitt of Harvard Business School, "creativity is thinking up new ideas," (Clifford, D.K., 1985). That was what RCA did 60 years ago. They began broadcasting radio programs to induce people to buy radios. Hewlett-Packard created demand for their computers with Kurtzig's software program for manufacturing management. Key Pharmaceuticals developed new ways to administer old medicines - Theo-Dur-time released into the blood stream for treatment of Asthma and; Nitroglycerin treated bandage for patients with angina pectoris. Lenox China created a market by promoting the bridal registry in America, where the bride picks her china pattern with the dealers; and friends and relatives, buy the parts of the set according to their means and disposition.

The creative process that generates new product ideas used to be poorly understood and poorly managed. Time and money traditionally went to product development, prototypes and testing; but not to brain storming, customer focus groups and other sources of creative new product ideas. That was until recently. Today, emphasis is placed on the very first stage of product life cycle, nurturing and evaluating new ideas within the companies.

Management is also responding to the fact that, with today's people and today's technology, command-and-contro1 no longer works best. Their approaches are changing, to seek employee collaboration across the organisation, to allow them to be more involved in the management of their respective activities, to permit them to professionally express their capabilities and to effect changes that contribute to the success of the business, to share risks and rewards; to gamer all human, intellectual and information assets, for creative use. What they look for are a set of values or principles which guide the employees' conduct in his (or her) everyday life and which directly motivates and inspires him (or her). Such values include personal life goals, concept of happiness, beliefs about what is morally right or wrong and social ideals. This has become all the more critical because of the current drive for globalization of free trade, while dealing with employees in different countries and different cultures.

Most profound changes in industry relate to what to expect from workers and what they expect from the job. Worker involvement and participation have become standard operating procedure. *Teams and teamwork* have become the basic units of management structure of many successful companies. Major issues like design, quality, cost, service, etc are now subject to teamwork for more effective solutions. General Electric Co., Motorola Inc., General Motors Corp., Toyota, Hewlett Packard, Boeing - the list of companies using team work as a routine is unending. From managing to leading and coaching, there has come about a maturation of the trend to leadership, communication and shared responsibility. That is not the limit.

The traditional, myopic view was that if one does his or her job, and does it well, he or she would get promoted to the next higher level. The harsh new reality is that those levels are fast disappearing. Peter Drucker, in one of his books, recommends seven layers as the maximum necessary for an organisation. Tom Peters insists on five. Kennametal is delayering from eight to five levels. A.T. Kearney, in their 1985 study, shows that the winning companies had less than four layers. Nucor has three in one steel plant. Semco, Brazil, has three tiers and four titles. The need for continuous improvement has triggered numerous work-design changes that are leading to blurring of job descriptions, elimination of distinctions, even between managerial and non-managerial work. Kellog, the world's largest cereal maker, has embarked on evaluating which white collar jobs are absolutely necessary and which are not. Pay and compensation structures are also changing, to reflect the changing work. *Results* count; not efficiency of work, nor narrow concerns of tenure, service seniority and job positions. Lifetime employment is crumbling. Promotions are no longer rewards for performance, but for ability. Industries like Sony are beginning to tie pay to results.

It is through innovation that leading manufacturers are able to design, make and deliver values - the right product, at the right time to that important right person: the end user.

Employees have begun to seek creative perquisites that improve quality of life and give more value for compensation.

We have only started to recognize the value that diversity can play in the work place. A group called PRISM, which stands for Pride, Respect, Individuality and Support, is one of three so called affinity networks operating at Mellon Bank, Pittsburgh, USA, for the past one year. The others are in leadership companies, like Smith Kline, GE, Xerox and Goldman Sachs. Networking makes it possible to be different and take a pro-active role. The members meet in corporate auditoriums or company sites, over coffee, lunch or dinner. Guest speakers address the meetings on various issues, like mentoring, business role models, how to cope with being in the minority within the corporation, etc. The networks attempt to provide advice and support to people with stressful issues; tackles traditional career and mentoring topics; find more effective ways to do the jobs; and become sounding boards for understanding the clients and specific cultures. It may be too early to gauge the result of such networks; but, they are worthy of emulation as a value adder.

BUSINESS REALITIES

The fundamentals of business have changed. A comparison of what it was in the past and what it is today, covers some important aspects. In brief, they are now *speed and flexibility,* instead of size and scale; *effectiveness,* in addition to *efficiency; team work and empowerment,* instead of command and control; *collaboration and sharing* information, instead of monopolising; contracting and *outsourcing* instead of self-sufficiency.

In the ultimate analysis, all business operations can be reduced to three Ps – People, Product and Profits.

Profits come from margins. Economies of scale (on which mass production at low cost was based) are becoming lower in worth day by day, because competitors can easily copy physical plant and equipment. Same is the case with patents: it is not difficult to find loop holes in the legal provisions. By selling millions of units, the production line can be refined to get the costs down and increase the margins. However, there is a limit. It would be too much to expect its extension to wipe out competition and monopolize the market.

Companies are led by humans and humans stray from premises that made a company great. All the same, people are all that is left. Realizing this, a major renaissance of responsible business and social transformation has begun. The mind set is shifting to focus on getting the best out of the people, building their capacity and capability, sustainability, cooperation, etc. Emphasis is now on retaining in service those in whom the tacit knowledge resides, training and developing them. The trend in training is *action learning.* It works. While people are learning, they are doing real work for the company. So, there is an immediate return on investment. It builds social net works, which are of value. It calls top management attention to promising stars. It forges and polishes talent. It is just-in-time learning.

Customers do not care about cost. They want cost's richer relation, value. They see themselves as buying value, or a solution to a problem. They are interested in more than the price. They are interested in their *total costs* of obtaining, using, maintaining, and disposing of a product or service. Companies can no longer raise prices in step with their costs. On the other hand, decreasing the price adds value to the item. Price depends on cost, which is directly related to resources used. Cost is incurred for a result. Therefore, what is important is the ratio of result to the effort that incurs the cost. To be cost effective, it will mean not only good cost control, and successful cost reduction drives, but more importantly, *cost prevention* or cost avoidance. Typically, costs are controlled, and, hopefully, reduced, through conserving resources, commonly understood as making do with less. Conservation is not synonymous with diminution of life style. It is synonymous with more wealth, more power, and more efficiency. The target is to *prevent unnecessary use of resources and unnecessary costs.* That is, to identify and eliminate (or to prune to the minimum) anything and everything that does not add value to the product or service. A source says 70 to 85 per cent of all work a company does is of no value.

Customer requirements and competitive forces have changed significantly every few years in the past. Global competitors are now an established fact. Staggering advances in transportation and communication are eliminating barriers to global operations and world trade. International Standards are an added fillip. Companies are operating nationally and internationally. Homogeneous specifications enforce homogeneous capabilities. Goods are made to paramount rating of six sigma, virtual perfection, with a defect rate of only 3.4 parts per million. Products have reached, or will soon reach, an equality of quality. There will no longer be any way to differentiate between them. They all meet standards - open, national and international - and would be traded freely: anyone can now buy or sell to anyone else, anywhere in the world. *To create relevant and distinctive product (or service) differentiation and to maintain it ever lasting,* companies have begun to search for the next advantage. Products of value were modifications, minor innovations, or major innovations. A recent study shows that they were in the proportion 70 : 20 : 10, respectively.

Companies are integrating across boundaries, becoming transnational (as opposed to multi-national), to take advantage of strengths in particular areas and offsetting weaknesses. *Collaboration* has become more efficient. They are building a net work of interrelated organisations that share product development, production, research and development, knowledge on technology and costs. Thereby, they gain advantages of skills; controls to improve quality; strategic issues to share resources; modes of distribution and marketing to reduce overheads; and means to lower costs. Automobile design teams are located in different geographic regions: the body in Italy, the engine in Germany, the transmission in Japan, etc. Armed with a digital design sped from somewhere in the world-wide system, a milling machine in say, Turin, Italy, could turn out a plastic foam model of a car, in no time. Visualisation techniques provide a way to investigate the potential of new designs, how the components will work, as well-as when assembled. Virtual reality enables manipulation to check for flaws or interference before actual parts are made. Major pharmaceutical companies now have research laboratories in five or six countries, but produce wherever the economies of scale dictate. Many car and airplane parts are made in half a dozen countries; stores sell look alike clothes sewn on four continents; money, stocks and bonds are traded on worldwide electronic markets. The drive is for *global sourcing*, for the most cost-effective mix of design, manufacture, supplies, components, transport and funds. It is today possible to borrow advanced ideas from one end of the world and make improvements on them at another. Products that were once expected to produce earnings for three to five years now last for a year or less. In the micro computer business, even less. Thus, firms, with years of technical leads, today find their products matched (not copied), reverse engineered and bettered by competitors in no time.

Top priority goes to *reduce the time from concept to customer.* For, the one who has the idea, but is incapable of converting that immediately into turn over, will lose out to someone else who might be better in doing that. A rule of thumb was a 20-year cycle to go from basic science to a commercial product; and 3 to 4 years, design concept to product. Computerised Product Development System (PDM) has already helped to shave almost 2 years off the 5 required for product development just a few years ago; and should eliminate 1 more with implementation of concurrent and simultaneous engineering practices. Manufacturing cycle times have declined from years in the past to months now. Many products are brought to market 9 to 12 months after start of work on them. Whereas it took 37 years for radio to get to 50 million homes, the web got there in four. The gestation period of 4 years and $ one billion in costs to get a car from the drawing board to the road and a life cycle of 4 years (7 for the first version) that were typical of an automobile are luxuries of the past. Honda can design a new car in 2 years and Ford in 30 months or less. Nobody can afford to make a car from scratch any more: it cost Ford $ 29 billion for designing its Taurus/Sable program. By putting the Caravan/Voyager on the already paid for K platform, Chrysler cut the cost of the program to $ 700 million. Biggest savings are in flexible manufacturing of 5 or more different kinds of cars on the same production line. This is done by balancing production between fast and slow moving models, hydro forming body parts, eliminating excessive redundancies and similar techniques.

Life cycles of many high tech products are now measured in months, instead of years. *Parallel development,* developing second and third or next any generation products, catalogue design, global sourcing, high tech and high touch have become the key. The natural consequence is escalation, more than ever before, of national and international competition in all products and services.

Success in international commerce cannot be accomplished by maintaining the status quo. To beat competition, improvements have to be at least a shade better than what the competition achieves. One excellent and relatively under used way is to seek creative insights in industries far afield from own and at apparently unrelated places. The real competition would include some of the allies - or even customers; not only producers of similar products and services. Once, the world was simple and so were relationships. Partners were allies. Competitors were foes. But, today, people one competes with one day, are partners, the next. Firms also see that they cannot compete alone in the world market. Logistics to improve the quality of supply chains are becoming an important part of business strategy. Therefore, they are linking themselves in *partnerships* with the suppliers and distributors. Above all else, to really improve and maintain an edge over competition, companies have to devote painstaking attention to the needs of the customers. There should be freedom to respond completely to these needs. It enjoins re-thinking on a fundamental level: what the current products (or services) are; what they do; what and where all the customers find *value;* and make improvements, quickly and profitably. Kennametal Inc., once a supplier of tool inserts only, transformed to *Total Customer Service,* by becoming a *One-Stop Shopping facility,* for all metal supplies and tools for its customer.

Time was when organisations were concerned with being. In the future, they will be concerned with becoming. One cannot throw away the company and start afresh. Nor can it be remade overnight. Nonetheless, companies that survive years from now, will be those that recognise *what is of value;* understand what they need to do to respond to *create, build,* or *add value;* make and communicate that change quickly and with direction; and do what they have to do, to re-align skills. As the first step, they should break out of the vicious circle of fire fighting, which is draining time, energy and money away from improvements. They have not only to think, plan and act on a truly global basis, but also to build around managing values and value enhancements, rather than managing physical resources. To illustrate, the chaotic debt ridden French Groupe Schneide of the 60s transformed itself into a $ 11 billion world electronics power that now generates 50 percent of its sales from international operations. It changed its concept to manufacture locally 95 percent products for world use and change the last 5 percent at the end of the process for use in a specific country – insted of conventional, all 100 percent in the country of sale.

MANAGE FOR VALUE

Building up a business to a certain level is comparatively simple. However, to survive, and exist, it needs more than designs, determination, and relevance: *value, in everything made and done.*

The quest to deliver value has been eternal. Because value means many things to many people, there were many areas for action. For some of them, different concepts, ideas, tools and techniques were, from time to time, developed and exploited with varying degrees of successes. These were good enough so far. However, these will no longer suffice, to survive, grow or prosper in the future. The spectacular developments now occurring in science and technology, world economy and trade, make imperative a *holistic approach to manage value.*

It will mean:

- *discovering ever more effective ways of turning knowledge and technology into useful products and services;*
- *creating change and managing change, exploiting every opportunity to create value;*
- *practical values flowing to the user and the customer in the most economical way;*
- *unique product or service of better customer perceived value;*
- *excellence from everyone and everything done;*
- *evolutionary improvement, continuous and continual;*
- *effectiveness* in addition to efficiency;
- *tops in core capabilities* in addition to good standards in others;
- *flexibility* in addition to uniqueness;
- *team work* in addition to individual contribution;
- team literally dissecting the product to the last element.
- *collaboration and partnering* in addition to cooperation;
- *cost prevention* in addition to cost reduction;
- *innovating to design, make and deliver value;*
- *helping employees to become more creative;*
- *creating relevant and distinctive differentiation;*
- *reducing time from concept to customer;*
- *applying classic management criterion: price-performance ratio;*

- *each look resulting in benefits, improving bench mark set earlier.*
- *preventing making a Rolls Royce product at ford price, or a ford at Rolls Royce costs.*
- *total service and one stop facility;*
- *kansei,* or in congruence with the community and natural harmony;
- *recognising what is of value; creating, building and adding value;* and
- *value in everything made and done.*

Lessons from The Best

- Early Period
- Mid Century and Beyond
- Recent Additions
- Examples to Emulate
- Lessons to Learn

LESSONS FROM THE BEST

2

Winning companies do not get to the top by accident. Their experience, truly, are the best teachers. How the winners achieved excellence, improved productivity, efficiency and quality in their plants, their strategies and practices could, and should, be role models. Some embraced new technology wholesale, while others preferred to adapt and add new technology to what was already existing. Some held people as paramount and sought improved industrial relations. Some improved by cutting costs and employees. Some went after big, crowded markets to enlarge their market shares, while others pursued over-looked and under-served markets. Some even created new markets. None had any simple set of directions for the road to success; or any formulae to apply. Yet, all their endeavors brought them to the same destination: the very top.

It took the winners a steady stream of concepts, ideas, strategies, approaches, tools and techniques to stay on the top of relentless waves of changes over time. Logically, it will need a continuing abundance of these to keep on winning, in the next millennium.

EARLY PERIOD

Large scale *assembly lines,* using similar components, was the invention of the Venice Shipbuilding Arsenal, in 1500, to *increase the size* of Vatican Navy, in times of war. The automobile industry lays store on this basic concept for the core of their operations. Moving assembly line brings the work to the worker for repetitive manufacture of standard items in large quantities.

Adam Smith (1776) brought craftsmen into the factory and divided the craft into discrete tasks that could be constantly repeated. He conceived that *division* or *specialisation of labour* increased production and *reduced levels of skill required* of workers. Today's airlines, steel mills, engineering firms, computer chip makers and accounting companies are all built around Smith's central idea.

With Eli Whitney (1798) making parts interchangeable, *standardisation* and *interchangeability* became, and continue to be, the bastions to *manage costs.*

Charles Babbage (1832) propounded the concept of *economies of scale,* yet another important tool for cost control. Annual drive for cost reduction is a predictive part of most businesses nowadays.

People started thinking about work design when Frederick W. Taylor (1890) wanted somebody to own and be masterful at a simple task. He showed that the real potential for increased output was to work smarter. He originated the idea of *scientific management* to analyse the operations involved in production, determine the tools necessary to do the job, and set standards for a day's work. He concentrated on job content, job method and fair wages.

Henry Ford (1900) capitalised on the idea of dividing work into tiny, repeatable tasks, to *mass-produce* automobiles and make it available to people, who previously could not afford them.

The Gilbreths (1910) contributed time and motion study, an analytical tool for studying the *methods and procedures,* timing them and measuring work. Alan H. Mogensen (1930) pioneered a series of articles on work simplification that brought this little used tool into lime light. Next, H. Gantt projected the operations against time, in his planning charts. M.P. Follett showed how workers' judgement and ideas could become part of production output. These helped work-study, work simplification, production control and payment by results. Current performance-, efficiency-, incentive-oriented approaches for management are extensions of these concepts. Work simplification and division of labour made possible mechanisation and improved production *efficiency.* Harold Maynard pioneered the concept of *method time measurement (MTM).*

In the post industrial revolution era, value was sought in *production* (what to produce, where and how); increasing *capacity* (to produce far more manufactured goods than ever before); and dramatically *lowering costs* (to raise wages for labour and add purchasing power for customers).

MID CENTURY AND BEYOND

Automation extended the capacity of machines to perform certain tasks formerly done by humans and to operate sequentially, independently or nearly independently of human control. Automation greatly *increased production and lowered costs.* In the same progression, robots are now changing the way we create and manufacture products, perform complex work activities, and clean up, including hazardous materials and waste.

With the concept of *synthesis and systems,* well-structured problems at tactical level were solved subjectively. The mathematical and quantitative approach relied on predictive mathematical models of systems and procedures.

The birth of *quality control* is generally recognised as 1924, when Walter Shewart first applied statistical principles at Western Electric's Hawthorne Plant (1924), to distinguish and chart variations vs. causes. He used it to analyse a process or its output so as to take appropriate actions to achieve and maintain *quality.* The early proponents of quality control were Shewart, Dr Edwards D. Deming, and Prof. M. Juran. Deming used statistical control methods in industrial processes to teach skills to people to achieve quality improvement. In ten short years, this approach yielded place to Total Quality Management (TQM). Focusing attention on processes that do not work, TQM system (1980) gathers data, looks for deviations, identifies cause and effect, and fixes the problem. TQM, led by the Japanese, has now become a pervasive part of current business thinking, the world over. It has caused the quality levels of many items to rise. Motorola adopted TQM in 1987 to achieve six sigma quality (3.4 manufacturing defects per million) within the next few years. It reaped cumulative savings of $ 4.5 billion from 1989 through 1993. During the same period, its selling prices declined 20 percent per year, while stocks appreciated over 400 percent. Hewlett Packard reduced production time of oscilloscopes by 30 percent; the cost of repair and servicing of desk top computers by 35 percent; and HP 3000 logic chip failure rate by tenfold.

Operations Research came out of World War II. James Kelly of Remington Rand and Morgan Walker of Du Pont (1957) developed the *Critical Path Method (CPM).* It was first used to improve planning, scheduling and coordination of its new plant construction efforts. *Program Evaluation and Review Technique (PERT)* was introduced on Polaris Weapon System in 1958, with the aid of Booz Allen and Hamilton.

The advent of the computer greatly facilitated the use of *feed back loops* in manufacturing processes. Truly bewildering is the plethora of ideas, tools and techniques using the computer. Among them, of note are Computer Assisted Design (CAD), Computer Assisted Engineering (CAE), Computer Assisted Maintenance (CAM), Computer Integrated Manufacturing (CIM), Computer Numerical Control (CNC), Virtual Reality (VR), etc. Increased computer power and development of information highway will soon facilitate face to face, real time, interactions among co-workers at separate locations, in different countries, or out-source a great number of tasks to super speciality, most efficient niche companies. Rapid manufacturing is the next step after virtual reality and rapid prototyping. Workers are likely to be wearing soon their computers, viewing information on face shields in front of their eyes and making instant decisions.

The Hawthorne experiments demonstrated that "productivity increased when a work situation was constantly attended to and stimulated," (Peters, TJ., 1988), focusing attention on the human side of enterprises. Behavioural scientists applied social and behavioural science to *motivation* (1940). Here, Henri Fayol, Walter Rathenau and Hugo Mcmunstenberg made their individual contributions: expanding work content, making it more interesting and challenging, making it something people wanted to do and something people could control. Concepts of Job Methods, Job Instructions, Job Relations, Job Safety, Job Classification, Job Enrichment, etc., were born. Peter Drucker suggested results-oriented approach.

Value Engineering (1950), the more effective value improvement technique, is the by-product of World War II efforts to maintain and increase production of all items against scarcity conditions. It is an organised, systematic, creative and common sense approach for solving problems, *continuous and continual improvement* of product and services, and/or *reducing costs,* while maintaining or improving performance and quality requirements. The product and performance improvements made in General Electric were Mile's contributions with this methodology. The early pre-fabrication techniques and faster and cheaper all welded design of Henry J. Kaiser, builder of Liberty Freighters, were value concepts. The design improvements adopted at US Navy Bureau of Ships for submarines were a sequel to Value Engineering training for the Navy engineers. The Airline system of "economy fares" to take up empty seats on scheduled flights was another value concept. The automobile industries all over the world and products produced in Japan are outstanding value enhancing accomplishments. Today, Value Engineering has evolved from the original purchase-based analysis method to an all powerful management-based system.

The period of prosperity in the later half of the 20th century witnessed production rises, employment, wages and profit increases, and investment expansions. Trade, commerce and competition escalated. The upswing also spawned some problems - increase in production costs, shortages of raw materials, energy crisis and price rises. Industrial priorities continued to be in *economies of scale and mass; efficiency, motivation and lowering of costs and prices.* However, these were additions, also of values, for the consumers to get the maximum amount and variety of quality goods and services they desire.

RECENT ADDITIONS

Traditional systems meant single purpose machine tools set in line to make a specific, standard product or part, in large quantities, at high speeds. It also required long set up times and frequent change over to achieve short runs of product. To meet the individual needs of the customers, came the refinement, Flexible or Agile Manufacturing, to *produce small lots and varieties, at affordable costs.* Apparel industry is leading the way in Agile Manufacturing. Quick fit tailors, at point of sale, measure and record the customer's precise body measurements with scanning devices. They also select style and fabric with him or her, convert the data to a two dimension pattern design on a computer and transmit by modem to the apparel manufacturer. The manufacturer matches the data received to a pattern existing in his computer and makes necessary fine adjustments. He relays the adjusted pattern to a high speed, single ply laser cutter to automatically generate the pieces for the customer. Routed then to a flexible, team-based production line, the apparel is stitched, packed and delivered express, to the quick fit tailor. In just four days, a custom tailored, right fit apparel is thus made ready, at a price comparable to the ready made, but ill fitting, off the rack, standard merchandise.

In the recent past, the noted author Richard Pascale advocated promoting positive conflict; and Eileen Shapiro, consciously shaking the status-quo; for achieving improvements. Bureaucracy, the *management structure and style,* with a rule for every contingency, lines of authority and reporting, that worked well for 100 years past, is followed by 90 percent of the enterprises. But, now Gifford and Elizabeth Pinchot diagnose it obsolete and forecast its replacement in the next 25 years by flatter, more lateral, more participative and power-down-the-line organisation. Their vision of the intelligent organisation of the future is one that uses the broader intelligence of *every employee,* and where real operational integration and teamwork take place.

The importance of getting the maximum contribution from every employee cannot be over emphasized. Increasingly, that is the only competitive advantage industry now has. Economies of scale are getting worth less and less everyday. Therefore, companies are considering seriously other strategies to make a difference. It is estimated that 5 percent of the employees are workaholics. Another 5 percent are at the other extreme: they wont work any better for any incentive whatsoever. It is the middle 90 percent that can be swayed with good motivational policies and practices. That is, good leadership, clear direction, reward for performance, enabling one to get the job done, cooperation, team work, providing an environment, treating with respect and dignity, and so on.

No one can afford a homogenous work force. Finding one is an impossibility. Diversity will be the rule. The hall mark of success is to get consistently superior performance from the diverse, non-homogenous workforce of average people. People make the difference: even one inspired person would do. It is the workforce that transcends the company, the industry, even the nation. They can change anything and everything: create new solutions, ask questions others would have never thought to ask, improve, challenge the limits, shatter convention, invent possibilities and innovate in a big way. Paying attention to people, giving them maximum opportunity to succeed, would realize the potential on which is hinged the success of every enterprise.

Evidence of what teams contribute is overwhelming. For good reason then, *teams and teamwork* have firmly taken root. At a survey of Fortune 1000 executives, half said they were converting to teamwork. The companies that thrive today are the ones that have learnt how to forge their various specialists into effective multifunctional teams. Giants like General Electric, Motorola Inc., and General Motors promote teamwork as a matter of course. In a typical example, Hewlett Packard employed a cross-functional team of representatives from procurement, manufacturing, packaging, distribution and logistics, (called it SPAM), to reduce the cost of their Desk-Jet-Plus line of printers. Their study revealed that HP could realise substantial savings by changing their mode of manufacture and supply of customised product. Earlier it was manufacturing the customised product at the factories and shipping the finished item to foreign customers. The change suggested was to manufacture the generic product at the factories, ship them and necessary components to distribution network abroad, and customise the generic product abroad to specific orders.

The 1991 Industry Week Survey of 340 US companies cites teamwork as the tool they use to solve major issues. Their fifth annual salute to America's best plants in 1994, quotes all the ten winners attesting their high levels of performance and competitiveness to their team approach to management and problem solving. At Martin Marietta Corp., 82 percent of the employees participate in self-directed work teams. They have trimmed manufacturing cycle time of water cooling system from 253 days to 126; and of antennas for radar in the Aegis system from 58 days to 29. Their scrap and defects in building an electronic module reduced by over 50 percent. Looking ahead, their targets for next year are: 50 percent improvement in assembly cycle time, 25 percent reduction in manufacturing costs, and 40 percent reduction in scrap and re-work. At Timken, Faircrest Steel Plant, a steel-processing quality team has achieved a 50 percent reduction in scrap segregation errors in just 2 months; a manufacturing cost reduction of 25 percent; and a maintenance cost reduction by 37 percent. Their technical study team has obtained a 50 percent improvement in reliability. Sony Electronics, San Diego, changed to a high performance work system based on participative management and self-directed team environment in 1989. That enabled it to become the most profitable and cost competitive maker of Trinitron Tubes.

Industry Week survey of Best Plants in USA, 1993 honours list, includes four companies. They are Honeywell, Unisys, Johnson & Johnson and Fisher Rosemont. Honeywell excelled with a world class manufacturing program (using custom-supply-solutions); Unisys, a total quality program (that extended partnership with customers and suppliers); Johnson & Johnson, a cross functional value analysis team; and Fisher Rosemont, a cross functional process improvement team. The most common characteristic of the 1995 winners, GE Electrical Distribution and Control Division, Milwaukee Electrical Tool Corporation, Rockwell International and Xel Communication Inc., is their emphasis on tapping employee brain power in a team environment. All of them used self-directed teams. Self-directed work teams are groups, not led by the Foreman, but by their natural leader, who decides how best to go about doing what they have to do.

With teamwork, Lars Kolind of Oticon Holding A/S, Denmark's highly successful, ultra-traditional hearing aid manufacturer, wrought a six fold rise in profits in 1992 and more than doubled it in 1993. It also made a wholesale transformation from a $ 27 million unit to a $ 436 million organisation.

Re-engineering, highlighted by James Champy and Michael Hammer, became 1993's premier performance improvement method. It swept the American management world with tornado speed, despite being considered a new label for the age-old ideas that should be practiced as a matter of course. Almost 95 percent of America's mid-sized industries have re-engineered at least part of their operation; and 30 percent, the entire business. It is the third most frequently practiced technique not only in USA, but all over the world. It is seen as a panacea for poor performance.

Done right, Re-engineering involves re-thinking and re-design of core processes to *optimise* work flows and productivity: and to achieve *improvements* in critical, contemporary measures of *performance,* such as *cost, quality, service and speed.* Re-engineering changes everything - jobs, skills, processes, and expectations. Re-engineering is essentially reconsidering the way things are done; processes and practices that have evolved over time; and perfecting the advantages gained in the past: such as quality, time to market and customer responsiveness – and effecting change. It is almost the promise on customer satisfaction. Worker is the key to Re-engineering. A genuine Re-engineering effort typically reallocates the workforce creatively, rather than just through lay-off.

Belfab started Re-engineering in 1986, when it redesigned its value-added chain from order entry to distribution. For Hallmark Cards Inc., Re-engineering was one of a litany of tools they used to reorganise since 1987, along with just in-time, short cycle time, quality and reduction in management layers. Taco Bell (Retail food), Capital Holding (Insurance) and Bell Atlantic (Telephones) are other companies who have used Re-engineering to achieve spectacular results. However, for all its success, sadly, Re-engineering has been a disaster. It has become the instrument of massive downsizing by the mindless and misguided for a fleeting fix for profits. Nearly 30 percent of US workers lost their jobs from 1990 to 1995 due to job cuts or company shutdowns, according to Cogenetics Research Group. Fortunately, the decade of corporate reign of terror seems to be ending. Job elimination was at the lowest level in 1997.

Empowerment is another leadership technique offered by management experts as a sure path into the 21st century. It is a sort of atomic pile radiating energy, but not aimed at anything. Management aims that energy in constructive ways, articulating only a clear vision of what to achieve, and enabling the teams and employees to make decisions and contribute. No more working in hierarchies, at least no organisation charts or squares everywhere; drop confrontation in favour of cooperation; give up being the boss and become more like a coach; ideas can be from anywhere, so search the globe; in their approach. However, the catch here is that empowerment without direction is chaos. Besides, one cannot achieve empowerment by simply giving the people the authority to make decisions. They need the skill sets and tools as well. To acquire these skill sets they have to get good, honest feed back and coaching. With accessible data, easy-to-use analysis and modeling tools, front line workers - when properly trained - will have sophisticated decision-making capabilities.

Semco, Brazil, is an example of participatory management and empowerment at their best. Their management programs are based on three fundamental values - democracy (participation), profit sharing and information. With participation they gave employees control of their work; by sharing profits, initiative to create wealth and make a difference; and through free and frank information dissemination, updated status on what is working and what is not. Their organisation is a circle, (not a pyramid), with three tiers and four titles. Decisions are voted upon. Employees are self-directed. They plan, schedule time and job content - jobs too important to delegate to staff. There is no bureaucratic arteriosclerosis - no norms, manuals, rules and regulations, job descriptions, audit of systems, security checks, nor store rooms. Production is in-house (who do about half of what they once did in-house), at company supported satellites and by a medley of employees, part-time employees, ex-employees and even people not connected with Semco. To keep expenses to the minimum, each one takes on more and more non-production tasks, as needed. Sales and profits are good; quality, excellent; and loyalty, high. An outstanding exception of a successful company in the most chaotic environment, Brazil, where, since 1990, about 28 percent of capital good manufacturers have gone bankrupt, and gross industrial product fell, in the last 3 years, by 14 percent, 11 percent and 9 percent, each year.

Bench marking has become popular as a tool to assess the performance gaps between "what is" and "what could be," to identify the best practice enablers to reach the target, and to implement action on specific areas needing improvement. It is a means for competitive comparison of strengths and weaknesses, but requires self-assessment, understanding and measurement of own processes. The goal is to raise company's operations to a performance level that equals or exceeds that of the best-in-class companies. A recent survey showed that 75 percent of the Fortune 500 companies practiced Bench Marking. *Better production and/or increased productivity, better product and/or product design, and cost reduction* are reported. Many, however, feel it is too early to evaluate the technique. Besides, if one key participant in the market creates a new bench mark level, it changes the target level. Motorola, IBM, Westinghouse and Xerox have used a variety of models of bench marking to achieve improvements.

Among other new recipes for sure success are Concurrent Engineering, De-engineering, Envisioning, Downsizing, Re-structuring, et al. Concurrent Engineering helped to do certain steps concurrently. Right sizing and Re-structuring were good up to a point; but, they alone are not viable long-term business strategy. Whereas, downsizing, de-cluttering, de-layering and divesting paid some dividends in the form of more productivity and competitive economy. However, it is people-centered and a *painful process of making improvements*. It is "denominator management to raise asset productivity ratios," (Prahalad, C.K., 1994). It is cost-driven and does not address systemic problems. In 1991 alone, as most US industries scaled back, 375,000 jobs were lost and the axe kept falling on the beleaguered workers. This was, with only less than 25 percent of the companies completing the task. Together, the Fortune 500 companies managed to cut 2.6 million jobs between 1984 and 1993. Re-structuring, Downsizing, Re-engineering, layoff - all intended to reduce costs and promote an efficient, lean organisation - are, certainly, not ways to motivate the survivors. They put process first and people last.

In the horizon is a VEC process, digitally controlled chemical molding system that can be operated at site, or via the Internet from thousands of miles away. This technology means that we can manufacture almost any product, anywhere, any time: not necessarily locating plants close to sources of raw materials or communication facilities.

Customer delight is emerging as the single powerful tool for achieving and sustaining competitive edge. Customer satisfaction derives from designing, making and providing products and services that meet and *satisfy as much of their needs and requirements as possible.* High customer satisfaction begets large market share, high employee satisfaction, productivity gains and high cash flow. For the customer, today's needs are yesterday's desires, and tomorrow's needs have not yet crystallised. It begets satisfaction when today's needs are well met; but delight when today's desires (tomorrow's needs) are anticipated and provided for before the needs become explicit. Customer delight comes from how well one is doing as their supplier, in terms of value. However, it is still another matter to make them raving fans, to make them brag about you and to make them your sales persons. For that, one has to build a relationship for life, anticipating the needs and providing for them before becoming explicit - even shaping them.

Tom Peters, author and management consultant, focused on the need for *excellence.* Toro, a lawn mower manufacturer, rose from brink of bankruptcy in 1980 to prosperity and world class status, using a "Pride in Excellence" program. Toro built a winning team through a combination of six *"people values"* and six *"performance values."* Super bowl winner football team, Green Bay Packers, had coach Vince Lombardi, well known for his relentless *"pursuit of excellence"* (and winning). Japan Steel's Oita works has its slogan "001" - for zero accidents, zero pollution, number one performance. Dick Abodo of Wisconsin Energy Corporation used DELTA (Develop Excellence through Leadership, Teamwork and Accountability) classes.

The recent additions of tools, techniques, technologies and resources that the winners apply and the ideas they use to motivate the human spirit is a saga of *multi-faceted pursuit of excellence, world class quality, and performance standards.* Again, a pursuit for values. All use either or all of known *productivity drivers, partnerships, and win-win alliances, Just-in-Time, Kaizen projects and Continuous Improvement programs.* Workforce strategies include employee *empowerment, use of work teams, and training.* They look to their customers long before they pull their products through design, manufacturing and marketing; and long before their products are in use. *Customer focus* begins with direct customer involvement at the front end of development, tracking orders through production operations and quality as judged by the end users.

EXAMPLES TO EMULATE

Eastman Chemical Co., USA, the 10th largest American chemical producer, won the Malcom Baldrige National Quality Award, for weaving quality improvement into the fabric of the company. They ensured top management involvement, team work and use of the classic

Deming PDCA (plan, do, check and act) sequence. 70 percent of Eastman customers rate the company as No.1 Supplier.

When Rolls Royce, the leading car maker for 89 years, suffered a loss of $ 150 millions in 1991 and 1992, the company reshaped using a combination of lean manufacturing practices, craft-enterprise concepts and multi-functional teams for everything from new product development programs to changes in manufacturing.

Gillette has outpaced its competition for decades, consistently cutting its manufacturing costs, while improving quality. The secret of their success lies in the constant stream of innovative products, continuous improvement and close linkage between product development and manufacturing: custom designing all and manufacturing many of their own production equipment. In spite of tighter specifications, they now operate comfortably metal stamping presses at 800 to 1200 strokes per minute (double the speed, years ago). Their cycle time for molded plastic parts average less than 10 seconds: much below former levels. Rejects, parts per million, are in single digits.

Lincoln Electric, maker of arc welding equipment, is a model of efficiency. It dominates the price-sensitive welding market throughout the world. It guarantees life time employment for workers who have been there for at least three years. Its assembly line workers get paid on the basis of how much they produce, plus a year-end bonus. It moves employees at will to various jobs; and puts employees first, customers second and the share holders last. The employees here are not unionized.

Ups and downs are natural in corporate life, but the key is resilience to bounce back from adversity. Then they become extraordinary long term performers. That is what 3M, Motorola, Ford, Merck, P&G, Boeing, J&J, GE, Marriott, City Corp; and HP Sure demonstrated. 3M tried many things; but kept what works. Motorola went in for fast cycle time, in production design discipline, flexible manufacturing, inventory and supplier management, for their quantum leap. Putting people before profits was magical at Ford. One time world leader in automobile industry (1930), Ford lost place to General Motors for most of the 20th Century. Now, Ford is trying to recover its top spot by concentrating attention on its people strength. For the next ten years, Ford will be spending $ 200 million, on amenities for their employees, to make them design and produce the best selling cars ever. The subsidised services would include 24-hour on site child care, summer camp and tutoring, recreation, SAT preparation, financial planning for retirees, assistance to shut-in-seniors, etc. Hewlett Packard is credited with creating the corporate culture of teamwork. Some of the other vital choices are having a set of core values, a well defined value system by which processes and procedures function and defining value of the products and services in customer's eyes. Combining academic thinking and industrial experience, selecting and using appropriate tools and techniques and striving to achieve a new level of operation (rather than concentrating on fire fighting) also yielded best advantages. No business ever prospered by focusing just on the problems.

The winners thought about the whole value delivery system.

THE BEST COMPANIES TO WORK FOR

Fortune brings out every year a list of Best companies to work for and shows a comparison with what their rank was in the previous year. The issue dated Jan. 8, 2001 lists 100 companies and gives their ranks during 1999 and 2000. An extract from this issue is given here:

	2000	1999
S. W, Air lines	4	2
Microsoft	37	21
Intel	42	65
Lens Crafters	48	82
Hewlett Packard	63	43

S. W. Air lines was the most admired company. Microsoft is a rank below; but Walmart was a rank above.

LESSONS TO LEARN

The plethora of ideas, concepts, tools and techniques were focused initially on production of goods and services in abundance, creation of capacities and maintenance of technical efficiencies. Thereafter, attention was concentrated on efficiency, productivity, quality, motivating, et al., to survive competition and exist. No element of the business system was exempt - neither procurement, nor product design, engineering, manufacturing, distribution, marketing, nor service. All through the years, containment of cost remained a persistent and important criterion. Cost reduction is a special, although limited, form of value improvement. Great ideas, concepts, tools, techniques and strategies: everyone of them. Powerful, too. Most have been in existence for decades; some, even centuries. They never die. The winners have used them: singly, or in various combinations, to outperform in every way that counts - efficient production, distribution, and end use of low cost, high quality goods and services to satisfy every human need and want. Winning apart, advancing technology, falling trade barriers and adoption of world standards, make their continued use an inescapable necessity for any industry to survive and exist. To prosper and grow, it will continue to need every one of them, as the solid foundation to build the edifice on.

It is noteworthy that all means exploited hitherto were some aspect of value, or the other, though not on its entirety. Great potential remains for exploitation in those aspects of value not yet covered, or partially covered. The eternal quest will be, to make profits, while creating and providing greater and enduring values to the customers, to meet their needs effectively, reliably and well. These are indeed great many new and difficult tasks. The tasks will become even more difficult as we progress; and, more will be required from, and expected of, the Managers, to *manage for value.*

There will be no factory of the future, nor management concept or plan, neither a single role model, for management to replicate to manage for value. Nevertheless, some things will be fundamental and universal. Such as:

1. The imperative to manage for *values* and provide progressively increasing *values* in every thing. The product and service should provide ever-increasing *value return* to the customer. The company or organisation should not only be the buyer of other *suppliers' values,* but also *supplier of values* to the customers served; and every one in the company, a *value adder.*
2. The *appraisal for value returns,* once every 3 to 5 years, from every product, every service, every policy, every system, every

practice, every individual, to garner unexpected successes, as much as to forestall unexpected failures: *value appraisal.*

3. The pressure to continue learning of new things and new techniques; and the demand for at least a basic familiarity with the instruments of high tech: *value-added knowledge.*
4. The compulsion to harness the innate capacity of the enterprise. To excel with what is already available; to continuously change; improve and innovate; to quickly respond to change in technology, markets and customer requirements; and to apply tools, techniques and ideas: the *value-added skills.*
5. The dedication needed to build a well trained, committed, empowered workforce; to tap whose talents in many different ways to try to meet the needs and requirements of the customers: the *value-added work.*
6. The ability to handle same or more work with fewer people and increasingly disparate work force, even free-floating, free-agent talents of skilled individual contributors. To coordinate work in own locations, or homes, or scattered in tele-commuting centers, on the road, or at the locations of the suppliers, contractors and strategic partnering allies. More use of technology to assist, flexibility, re-structuring, and so on: the *value-added flow of the entire enterprise.*
7. The predominant search for, and creation of, integrated value chains linking not only the various areas within the company, but also outside the company, to customers, suppliers, distributors, and channels: building a network of inter related organizations that share detailed cost and technology knowledge and act effectively as a single unit: the *value-added alliances,* and
8. The performance measure basing your earnings on how much value you add - what you can create yourself, individually; what you can create as a member of the team; what you can create for your company, the customer and the society: *value you add.*

VALUE

Knowledge, technology are at the core of everything— everything of Value

- An Age Old Concept
- Many Meanings
- What is Value?
- Product (or Service) Value
- Customer Value
- Function and Value
- Quality as Value
- Cost as Value
- Design as Value
- Time as Value
- Summary

VALUE 3

In the companion book, *Value Engineering,* a chapter is devoted to the concept of value. Some additional explanations are contained in this chapter. Taken together, it will help to understand the concept better and make the discussion complete and comprehensive.

AN AGE OLD CONCEPT

Value is an age old, abstract concept. It is a goal of everyday life and something that we all seek.

The Greeks believed that value is an indwelling property of goods and services. That idea of value dwelling in goods and services still pervades our thinking. However, it is also seen as a force that governs our behaviour. It is centered in the people and the goods and services that they desire. Changes in their needs alter the value of the goods and services.

Aristotle, more than two thousand years ago, described seven classes of Value: Economic, Moral, Aesthetic, Social, Political, Religious and Judicial.

Perhaps, value is best understood from *Bhagawat Gita.* Chapter XIII, verses 7-11, enumerates twenty *values* that Krishna, the God incarnate, teaches Arjuna, a human hero. Though part of an important text of religious beliefs and norms of human behaviour, they constitute the basic determinants of much of our material world decision making. As Swami Dayananda Saraswathy eruditely explains, value here means "*the regard for a thing, situation or attitude, which, for some reason, is esteemed or prized by the value-holder.*"

Thing includes product, service or communication, those that can be seen, touched, felt or handled. They all have value. They derive value from their inherent properties and characteristics: like, life, performance, use, strength, composition. weight, configuration, etc.

Situation includes subjective attributes: like, ability, capability, condition, capacity, circumstance, position, location, context, quality, reliability, complexity, simplicity, intricacy, equality, congruence, surfeit, abundance, dearth, scarcity, rarity, harmony, suitability, interchangeability, maintainability, reparability, serviceability, possibility, probability, feasibility, manoeuvrability, etc.

Attitude is mental, emotional and ephemeral: like, appropriateness, desirability, difficulty, facility, ease, comfort, euphoria, delight, pleasing, esteem, etc.

By *value-holder* is meant the recipient. Value can be built into any item; but it is in its use that value thrives. Value is what the recipient gets out of what one receives.

It is value that gives direction to the development of norms.

MANY MEANINGS

The term "value" was, and is, used by many people, in many ways, to mean many things, in many contexts (Fig. 3.1).

The wide scope of definitions permits its extensive use. Dictionary meanings include: worth, a fair equivalent, esteem, efficacy, excellence, that which renders anything useful or desirable, and so on.

The customer defines value, if he or she has the economic power to improve his or her choice of acquiring or not acquiring. Otherwise, the producer defines value in terms of characteristics or features the customer is willing to pay for.

When used to indicate subjective qualities (styling, appearance, contour, shape, etc.), determined by emotions, the term "value" is not easy to define. However, when applied to indicate objective qualities, (like life, performance, reliability, weight, etc.), determined by properties and characteristics, it is measurable and quantifiable. A variety of factors influences these perspectives. Because these perspectives are dynamic, value changes over time.

Value of an item is a function of its importance and cost. That is why Economists define value as the *worth* of a commodity or service. Essentially, it means the *price* for which an item will sell. Whereas, Daniel Bernoulli, in his essay, the "Papers of the Imperial Academy of Science in St. Petersburg," suggests that the value of an item must not be based on price, but rather on *the utility that it yields.* Jevons, in *"theory of political economy"* concurs, but holds that *value depends entirely on utility.*

Carlos Fallon, in *"value analysis to improve productivity"*, (Fallen, C., 1971), expands the idea of utility as:

- The state of being *useful or serviceable,* as a farm tractor;
- *Fitness* for a given purpose, as an engagement ring;
- *Aptness* for a given application, as a parachute;
- *Beneficial* for a given condition, as aspirin;
- *Timeliness* in meeting a need, as a baby shower;
- *Suitability,* as an oasis; and, in summary, completing the cycle,
- The capability to *satisfy wants.*

I would like to add to this listing, *just right,* as fish and water.

Bradley T. Gale saw value as "simply *quality,* however the customer defines it, offered at the right price." By quality, he covered all non-price attributes of a product, including after-sales service and convenience of purchase (Gale, B.T., 1994).

Lawrence Miles, the originator of Value Engineering methodology, considered "a product or service to possess good value, if it has the *appropriate performance and costs"* (Miles, L.D.,1972).

To Rubber Maid, value is a combination of four inseparable attributes - *quality, price, service and speed.* For McDonald's, it is *what you get for what you pay.*

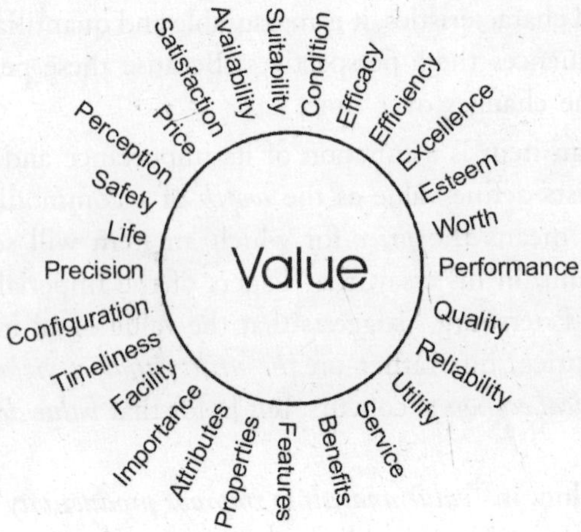

Fig. 3.1

When a work of art is purchased its value is derived not from the visible work; but from its invisible associations. The source of value of the item lies in its age (antiquity), rarity, historic connections, and even its cultural bias.

WHAT IS VALUE?

Value is a relationship, established by comparison. Christopher Barlow of North Western University holds that "value is about discovering relationships among the various goals of those who affect and are affected." Value is about performance compared to needs; intent compared to performance; needs compared to requirements; requirements compared to features or attributes; features or attributes compared to price and price compared to satisfaction. In general, value increases with higher use, esteem and exchange values; but decreases with higher cost value.

Fallon amplifies this with what John Stuart Mills called "difficulty in attainment," in his treatise on Principles of Political Economy. "That a thing may have any value, it must be of some *use* and it must satisfy some *desire.* Besides, there must be some difficulty in its acquisition, possession or attainment. When something is both desirable and difficult to get, someone has a problem (the user); and someone else has an opportunity (the producer). The item is made and sold to the user for the difference in difficulty in its acquisition, possession, or attainment. The difference between what the item means to the customer (worth) and what he or she has to pay for it (price), is the measure of customer value for the item," (Carlos Fallon, 1971).

"Value enhances with increasing performance, if and only if, the customer needs, wants, and is willing to pay for, more performance," (Miles, L.D., 1972).

Company performance, product performance and service performance are measured in terms of value added. The value of a product or service depends on controllable internal factors. Which are: materials (functional ability, producability, reliability), performance (primary function, secondary function), methods and procedures of production and execution, design specifications, skill and expertise, etc. The value also depends on applied situation, external to the company. Which are: channels and logistics, competition, market demand, vagaries of the supplier, needs of the consumer, etc.

Process and process technologies are often dictated, partly by scale and partly by product characteristics. Trade off between alternatives is made in terms of their projected performance and costs.

PRODUCT (OR SERVICE) VALUE

A product is the tangible object a customer buys. A service is the intangible result of the efforts of someone else. They both provide some benefits or returns, desired by the customer, to meet a need, or to solve a problem. If value is increased, the demand for the product or service increases, all other things being equal.

To provide the benefits or returns, many attributes and features are required. A product or service with the right attributes (use, esteem, cost and exchange) for the needs will be of value to the customer.

Take, for instance, safety in cars; and the attributes and features, added from time to time, to provide safer cars. The all-steel closed body was introduced in 1923. Floating power came in 1931. Safety padding was added on back of front seats in 1931. The safety rim was a 1941 development and padded dashboard, in 1950. A series of brake refinements, from four-wheel hydraulic brakes, air-cooled brakes, to anti lock brakes, were added between 1924 and 1971. The four-wheel drive that came in 1973 is now common for all cars. Last year, Mercedes

Benz, renowned for its rigorous safety, agreed to change tires on some cars and add new electronic controls, to counter rolling when swerving violently - a remote possibility revealed in a "moose avoidance manoeuvre" test. All were necessary and beneficial to the customer.

In the case of transmission, the progression was from H-slot gear shift (Packard, 1902), to synchromesh gears (Cadillac, 1928), column mounted gear shift (Pontiac, 1938), clutchless hydramatic drive (Oldsmobile, 1940), power glide (Chevrolet, 1950), push button automatic (Chrysler, 1956), Hurst shifter (1970), four speed over drive (1987), and the latest electrically shifted Tiptronic. More women are now buying cars and they prefer automatic transmission because it is easier to drive.

Nobody purchases a Rolex watch merely for its utility function (to show time). It is more for its adding esteem and its high exchange value.

Enhancing attributes or features will raise the value of the product or service, only if such enhancement in attributes and features are necessary and more beneficial. The value change of the proposed enhancement will depend on its additional merit (performance) and difference in cost. If the added cost results in a performance level not otherwise attainable, and this performance level makes the product better in whatever way the customers want, the value is increased. If not, even if the performance exceeds the requirements of its application, the value is lowered.

To illustrate, today's Laptop has to satisfy many needs with solid offerings, but for least money. Some customers need functionality and dependability. Some seek a variety of features, like fast processing, high-end video circuitry and top quality audio. Some are happy to forgo the fastest processor or the biggest display, to get a versatile machine. Some others, especially those who travel a lot, dragging gear through airports and bus stations, want it to be the smallest and lightest possible. Still others need a machine with all the features of a desk model, but one that does not occupy much space. However, all just want the best they can get for the least money.

Another example: sale of detergent "Surf" boomed in Indian villages, when small quantities were packaged for retail sale. Cost per packet became affordable to the poor villager.

Any transaction is an exchange of two things (say a product for money, or a service for a price). It also involves some use or intent of use (of the product or service) and some amount of satisfaction (derived or expected from the use). Value is that perceived difference, between one product (component, or brand) and another, which enables the customer to decide to purchase. This difference is due, partly, to scientific reasoning; and partly, otherwise, influenced by abstract forces - something imagined, something emotional and something ephemeral.

The customers "will not pay for value that they do not perceive, no matter how real it may be," (Porter, M.E., 1985). Their perception may differ from what the company offers. The product or service of perceived value will be in good demand. Customers may seek and search for it and even wait for it (if stocks are not available). When the product or service has earned fair perceived value, it will maintain and enhance its market share of loyal users. It may also attract some vulnerable users, become a global presence, or a monopoly. The measure of satisfaction provided by the product or service is the customer perceived value. For, if the price or the money paid is higher than this perceived value, there will be no exchange and transaction. This will explain the importance of application support to make the customer appreciate the real value of the offerings.

Since profits are truly the rewards paid to the company by the customer in return for real values, the products and services, made and provided, should be of the greatest value to the customer. Once understood, the company can apply all ingenuity to re-design the product or service, re-engineer equipment, process and systems, re-shape strategies, activities and functions, etc., to suit. The goal is to make the customers perceive the enhanced product or service as the best: like lowest cost compared to competition; highest performance (or service, or quality, or differentiation); etc. Not merely as one among the best, but *the best.*

Value should be the sole determinant for enhancing attributes and features: where, when and how much. The questions to be answered are:

- Is the enhancement need-based?
- Will it upgrade the product (or service) to leading edge?

- Will it contribute whatever constitutes better performance: size, shape, colour, weight, quality, reliability, durability, ease, etc.?
- Will it simplify, add flexibility, increase responsiveness, etc.?
- Will it improve aesthetics, sales appeal, features that inspire, etc.?
- What other differential will it improve?
- Is it the best, optimum combination?
- Is it customer-friendly, customer-intimate?
- Will it squeeze cost and waste out of company's processes?
- Will the delivered cost be lower than that of the competitors?
- Will it add new levels of customer service?
- Will it help customer improve productivity, upgrade his people's skills, apply the product better, solve customers' problems, etc.?
- Will the customer become more profitable?
- Will it need additional equipment, competencies or skills to make the change?
- What part of the past can we use as a lever to accelerate the change?

Value should also become the criteria for investment schedules, resource allocation, shares and priorities.

Service companies should look for optimising efficiencies at the customers' end and maximising operating efficiencies internally. Operating efficiencies relate to repeatability, experience, integrated cost and quality control, matching localised or individualised customer needs and recapturing customer use and operating patterns.

Therefore, it is of critical importance to understand the value that the customer places on the product or service, in order to create, build or add value to the product or service.

CUSTOMER VALUE

Value is not only what you build into your product and services, but also what the customers get out of you, your products and services.

Customer value is in the set of benefits sought. Often there is a core need, some primary, over-riding desire for accomplishment or satisfaction. There may be a series of additional, supplementary needs. The product or service presents a solution to the core need. The degree of satisfaction, however, may vary. Similarly, the attributes in the product or service may mix and match the supplementary needs in different combinations. Value results from the customers' perception of the total satisfaction provided by the product or service.

Customer satisfaction is also a measure of applied values. Not what you design, engineer or build into the products or services. Value is value in use: the way customers use the product or service in their operations, their functions, their processes and for their benefits; at the point of application and implementation. Value is knowing and applying ones products and services to generate revenues and profits for the customers and maximising it. As a corollary, applications functions must become the new value adders. Applications support will go to bridge the gap between the offering and the value the customer realises from it.

Customer value lies in his or her critical success factors. These comprise productivity increases, performance, life and quality-reliability improvements, larger profit margins, time and labour savings, bigger market shares and competitive advantages. Value from you, as the added competitive advantage to customers, could be in anyone or more of the following forms:

1. As reliable and consistent producer. For, dependable performance will be better than alternating cycles of superior and inferior performance.
2. As a quality and lower cost supplier. For, then only, your contributions can guarantee the stability and consistency of the customers' output. It, in turn, will really assist the customer to maximise volume, ensure productivity and manage cost-intensive problems.
3. As an associate, to accelerate the customers' most critical profit generators, raising margins and earnings. This can happen only with deep insight into the customers' operations: applying ones products and services to generate profits for the customers; and maximising it.
4. As a partner for profit, performing jointly with the customer your

development work at your end and problem solving for the customer at the customer's end, fast: even if only in enlightened self-interest.

Every critical success factor is inter-linked to one or more other factors. It is important to maintain synergy and avoid all adverse influences.

Therefore, it is of equal critical importance to understand the inter-connections and influences: why, where, what and how much.

Value is what is acceptable to the party (customer or user). In other words,

$$\text{Value} \sim \frac{\text{Worth} + \text{Want} + \text{Need}}{\text{Cost}} \tag{3.1}$$

Quantifiable product related values are:

(i) Function to price relationship;
(ii) Product features and benefits;
(iii) Quality reliability;
(iv) Life; and
(v) Performance.

Quantifiable service related values are:

(i) Warranty;
(ii) Repair, recall, replacements; and
(iii) Training.

FUNCTION AND VALUE

For an industrial Engineer, a product is an assembly of elements. For a Value Specialist, it is a means to the end of providing a function.

It is this magical concept of *function* that is at the core of the method of Value Management. It is not merely *"the action for which a thing exists"* which is what the dictionaries define. In fact that is how everybody understands the term. For Value Management, *function* means *"the essence of action for which the thing exists, expressed in two words (and not more) - one verb and one noun."* When possible, the verb should be demonstrable on a non-verbal level and the noun should be a parameter, or measurable quantity. Function (F) is defined as "that which makes a product work or sell" (Mudge, 1989). It is the natural or characteristic action performed by the product or service. Also, it is seen as the intended operation of the item, in its normally prescribed manner.

An item is of value if it accomplishes the function for which the user intends it. It is built at a cost (C). Therefore, the relationship:

$$\text{Value} \sim \frac{\text{Function}}{\text{Cost}} \text{ or } V \sim \frac{F}{C} \tag{3.2}$$

Value (V) derives from accomplishing the required function(s), by any means, but effectively, reliably and well. The customer or user is specially interested in the accomplishment of the necessary or required function. He or she is also interested in accomplishing it effectively, reliably and well. However, he or she does not care how it is accomplished. There exist numerous possibilities of accomplishing the function. Each possibility has a corresponding cost (see Fig. 3.2). Anything done to enhance the functional capacity and capability will increase the value, cost remaining the same, or increasing marginally.

The customer or user is not interested, neither do they care, about what else the product (or service) does. To the customer, anything additional, be it in primary functions or in secondary or support functions, are neither meaningful, nor important. Whereas, they are, and should be, to the producer, who incurs costs to provide these extras. Therefore, the importance of finding the point of balance: just right, neither less, nor more. "Anything more is unnecessary and wasteful. Anything less is unacceptable" (Tufty, 1983).

Value is also derived from providing the required functions or services at the desired time and place and with the essential quality.

Note that use value and esteem value are related to the physical properties that make a product (or service) satisfy the customer. Exchange value is related to its economic characteristics.

QUALITY AS VALUE

Siemens's quality motto is: "Quality is when our customers come back and our products don't." How true!

Quality is value to the extent it directly relates to performance. It may add to or detract from performance. A poor quality item may not meet performance requirement. Value increases by increasing price - performance, for the same cost or less.

The customer views quality as value in three situations: when obtaining a required level of quality at least cost; or highest levels of quality for a given cost; or an optimum compromise between the two. Conventionally, a quality product is that which works exactly as designed. The customer may not consider additional improvements to be of value. Quality superiority would not interest the customer, if he or she cannot get value out of that quality level. The measure of value is what and how much one's quality superiority confers on the customers' competitive advantage, benefits and satisfaction. With defects being now measured in parts per million, customers are unlikely to perceive defects, let alone direct improvements in the defect rates. That is not to detract from actions to control defect rates. For, with the acceptance of International Standards, a high level of quality has become mandatory. It cannot be escaped. Quality enhancement programs will continue to result in some value (internal benefits). like reducing direct labour on line, introducing new technologies faster, reducing costs, etc. Whereas, using internal norms of quality, companies change, add or delete heavily on features and attributes. These change quality correspondingly, but may affect costs (and price), without benefits or customer value.

Conventional approach is to offer high quality, lower priced products and services; or required quality at least cost. The real value solution is to optimise on both quality and cost. Whenever product parity is the rule, the price-performance merits of most products and services have a role in making them competitive.

COST AS VALUE

As seen from the formula (see Eq. 3.1), cost being in the denominator, anything done to decrease the cost, other things being the same, will improve value.

A product is a bundle of attributes and features in some configuration, shaped so by the conceptual, technological and physical application of activities in the company. It helps to differentiate the product or service: even make it unique. Any change in any of these factors will create or destroy value for the customer. However, substantial savings result from eliminating unnecessary attributes and features - especially those imposed by the overall design concept. So also from correcting inappropriate materials, ineffective methods of production and handling, etc. Determination of their contribution to the required performance (cost per function) of the finished product or service is the key. One can win by giving more or equivalents at same or lower costs and more for marginal increases in costs in the hope that the added costs are really creating values. Using internally generated measures of performance and efficiency, companies make changes, routinely, in one or more of these factors, with little or no regard for their effect on cost. On the other hand, the aim should be to maximise value at minimum cost.

A rule of thumb would be to apply Pareto's law to investments for enhancing attributes and features. The first 20 percent of the investment generally yield 80 percent of the benefits. The more one invests beyond this point, there would be only marginal gains. The law of diminishing gains governs the added costs beyond this limit. By knowing the customers' values, it should be possible to check and ensure that most of them fall within this limit.

The customer exchanges money for the product or service, if it is of good value. He or she interprets its value as good if it satisfies the need or solves the problem, effectively and well, at low cost.

His test will be to find if it is low, as compared to:

(i) what he or she had estimated to pay; or,

(ii) what he or she was willing to pay; or,

(iii) cost of alternatives available (from competitors or otherwise).

Anything done to reduce the cost, without adversely affecting the performance capability will increase the value of the product or service. Razor thin margins make cost containment a major focus in any industry. At the core is holding down costs on repetitive tasks, identifying and elimination of hidden costs and costs of business complexity, lower productivity and ineffective systems.

Performance can be related to the function, product attributes and features, life, quality and reliability. Similarly, service can be tied to repair, recall, replacements, application training and warranty. These relationships are quantifiable. For a function, there are several combinations of design concept, material, process, etc. - each with its cost characteristics. The choices are very many, as will be seen from Fig. 3.2. We may not be using less material-intensive means of creating economic value. We may also not using productivity as a cost saving measure in operations. But we can compare the ratio of resultant performance (RP) to resultant cost (RC) and rank numerically. Starting with the highest ratio, the possible routes to achieve a function can then be investigated and the feasible, best alternative lowest cost, chosen. It will seldom be the one in current usage. A change to the chosen alternative will yield cost advantage and corresponding improvement of value.

There are several ways to manufacture, to machine parts, or to create shapes. The same part can perhaps be made on different machines and a number of processes. Each permutation and combination will have a resultant cost (RC). Fig. 3.2 is limited to three materials and three processes. There could be several. Value enhancement here comes from action on the denominator (C) in the equation for value (Eq. 3.2).

The scope to improve value through cost containment is enormous. With guidance from Ford, Mazda has trimmed costs. Mazda was engineer-driven. Ford executives reviewed Mazda's free wheeling engines. They forced Mazda to share auto platforms and source many more items from overseas. With the result, the guidance became one of taking out costs to offset the loss in resources.

Miles showed that about 25 percent of the cost of any item are unnecessary. If the products were a rush issue, then, the figure could go as high as 50.

What is purchased from outside the company constitute 60 percent to 70 percent of the cost of the final product. These could be for materials, semis, components, services, etc. The hidden cost here is for waste.

There are three 20-80 rules, generally applicable to all cost structures. Fixed Cost to Variable Cost is in the ratio of 20 to 80. Approximately 20 percent of the parts contain 80 percent of the cost. In most assemblies, 20 to 30 percent of the parts (or costs) perform the Basic Function and 70 to 780 percent of the parts perform Secondary Functions.

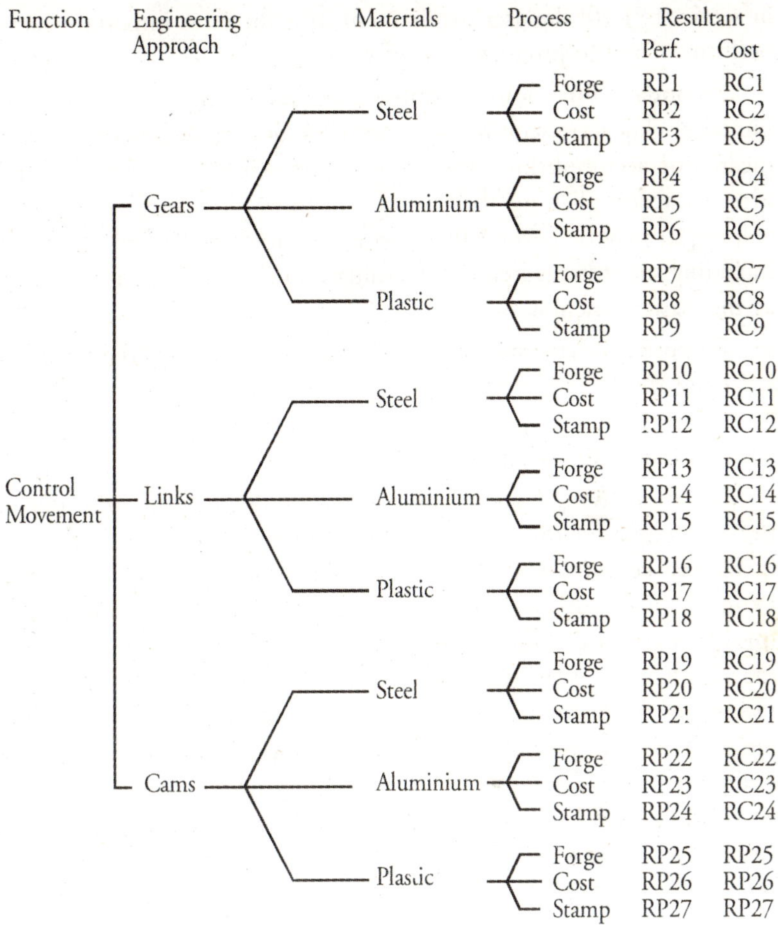

Fig. 3.2

Note:

- The permutations and combinations possible are several.
- Other engineering approaches are cable, chain and sprocket, etc.
- Other materials are copper, brass, etc.
- Other processes ares molding, extruding, etc.
- The alternatives are x^n.

Basic Function is that which is essential to the performance of the primary purpose, the utilitarian characteristic or feature of the product or service to fulfil the user requirement. It is the most important action performed by the product or service.

Secondary Functions are those required to implement the Basic Function. They are required to cause or allow the designer's choice of means for accomplishing the design approach chosen. They are not directly accomplishing the primary purpose, but supporting it, or helping it; may be beyond that needed to satisfy minimum user needs including superfluous items. A Secondary Function is not as important as the Basic Function.

Opportunities to improve value occur from improving the functions, reducing the Secondary Functions and/or incorporating the needed Secondary Functions into the parts that perform the Basic Function, with corresponding decrease in costs.

Greatest savings would come from secondary functions and no better example for this can be had other than *automobiles.* By the turn of the last century, most American families had two cars ; some three or more. The market became crowded with better performing, high quality cars and from a number of national and international manufacturers. Simultaneously, the prices got bigger each year. However, the customers could not, and would not, pay that kind of money for a car. Since Henry Ford introduced his version, there has been no break-through, changing the primary function of the automobile from being a person or material mover. That being so, over years, the secondary functions had multiplied and diversified - style, six way power driver's seats, fender skirts, semi-automatic starter, chrome chips, sculpting, cup holders, keyless entry, sound system, leg room, rear seat climate control, dash board design, arm rests, power windows, delay wipers, alloy wheels, homogenous designs and so on. Drivers now expect their cars to do more than simply start in the morning and get them to office. They want to feel pampered when stuck in traffic. They are asking for ambience and emotion. They want everything where they expect it to be; and it must feel, sound and smell just right. Everyone of them is a secondary function and cost money to provide.

Another big expense is overheads, which are about 35 percent of the total cost. Cut out the overhead fat continuously and rigorously. Almost 15 percent to 20 percent of the overhead go to errors, recovery from errors and rectifying mistakes. So also the marketing gimmicks: discount coupons; buy one, get one at 50% (or free); whole sale/ warehouse club; etc. These represent costs, but not any value addition. Overheads merit attention in preference to direct labour, which accounts for only 15 per cent.

As a major component of the cost pie, in service functions and non-critical items of lower value, there are ever so many other ways in which value can be used to save on costs. Intrinsic to it are the possibility of reducing any job to a routine work and describing it in a specification; and of replacing any function being done in-house with a third party work or contract. Technology would accelerate the transfer. The only relevant issue would be the cost. Most vulnerable areas are the support, ancillary and mandatory tasks. Such work could include customer services, retailing, transportation and every office job-billing, accounting, analysis, data processing, transcriptions, etc.

Pay for high performance. On the shop floor, relate the high pay to higher value added. A car door, built in Japan, costs half that built in USA. The difference is not due to lower labour costs in Japan. Almost 75 percent are caused by the difference in design, blanking and stamping, and scrap generated. Of the rest, 25 per cent is due to difference in the number and complexity of components, type of material and unnecessary performance margins. U. S. Air, America's seventh largest air line struggles to survive a second bankruptcy. It hopes that lower labor costs would enable it to compete with discount carriers. The correct reaction to lower price competition is not a matching lower price. The healthier reaction must be to provide in the product or service:

- greater value, or
- more quickly realised value, or
- more certain value.

DESIGN AS VALUE

When products are equal in price and functionality, design is another differential that matters. Especially, during current times, when prosperity and technology are at cross roads with culture and marketing. Manufacturers recognize that consumers are looking for more than functional benefits. Customers place a premium on esteem value: they will not buy the product unless it adds psychological and emotional benefits. These benefits are sought through design styles, shapes, etc. This philosophy is seen reflected in the pattern of toothbrushes - ridged, twisted, tapered, with bands, dots and swirls. So also, in other mundane items, such as garbage cans, toilet brushes, and vegetable graters. Only, in making them cute, colourful, stylish and disposable, the products have to be affordable also.

In a majority of items, the cost of the design work (and committed through design into product cost) was assumed to be around 75%. However, in the last few years, this has crept up to almost 85 %. As this happens much ahead of the item going into production, some changes are being tried on some items. Traditionally, manufacturers do most of the work for product development, bearing the cost and time needed for the iterations between themselves and the customer to reach a satisfactory solution. The *need* information (what the customer wants) is with the customer. The *solution* information (how to satisfy those needs) is with the manufacturer. The customer needs are often complex, subtle and fast changing. They do not fully understand, nor articulate well, their needs. They often prefer to see and try out prototypes, to explore what does and does not work. In fact, they even solve the problem. Letting the customer innovate increases speed and effectiveness; also by-passes the expensive and error-prone effort. Three suppliers market: one of specialty flavors to companies like Nestle, etc.; of computer chips; and of resins to plastic manufacturers; are experimenting to make the customers innovators. They are providing the customers with tool kits that enable the customers to develop their own combinations (design task), make samples (or simulate), quicken iterations (learn by doing), reduce development risks (savings) and enhance customer base (value).

Design is not the province of engineering, not even engineering and manufacturing, jointly. Instead, representatives of every stage in the product's life cycle, from materials employed in its production, to its ultimate disposal, participate in setting its design specifications. The tool of choice for the designer is three dimensional solid modeling, which allows instant insight into the proposed creations. Then, it is easier to know what to change.

Concurrent engineering reduces product development time, by doing certain steps concurrently, eliminating the traditional build and test merry go round. It also makes possible a higher quality product at a lower cost. Visual reality enables manipulation and assembly of parts on screen, before actual parts are built, to check for possible design flaws or interferences.

The quest is never ending to make the product or service meet better the user's requirements. Therefore, companies design for the users, with the users - and even let the customers take over. The classic example is IKEA.

TIME AS VALUE

Faced with more than 28 hours' worth of daily tasks, time management has been the subject of great attention. Programs and gadgets abound to plan, schedule and more effectively use every moment of the working day.

Technology has provided some answers to squeeze added value out of each nano-second. To wit, the cell telephone that enables making business contacts while commuting; the internet that allows answering e-mails from wherever in the world one happens to be; the voice mail that leaves messages; the video conferencing for one-on-one or one-on-several meetings; and so on. These enable one to multi-task, re-allocate free time and so on.

Taking time out of one's hectic schedule for self-improvement would dramatically improve his (or her) effectiveness.

Juggling work and home is a joy, as well as a challenge. Certain amount of time management is necessary for modem life to work at all. However, concentrating intently makes one lose track of time and does not help to get the day to day triathlons of business needs. Therefore, value is not in micro-managing time. Real value derives in securing a psychic state, called "Flow." This is the state in which people are most competent, productive and creative. It is when one would be absorbed by what is being done and become euphoric.

In this age, when almost everyone feels time stressed, companies must find ways of doing business that reduce hassles. They could avoid such things like:

- Making one come in for meetings, when a telephone call could suffice.
- Come twice (or more), when one visit would suffice.
- Fill out forms, working round cumbersome processes.
- Slogging through pages of instructions.
- Waiting.

Whether companies launch new products, or introduce new features, or customized versions of existing products, their battle cry is the same: be first to market. If they succeed, they would be seen as progressive, innovative, understanding of the customers' needs and meeting them more effectively. They would be capitalizing on their knowledge for product introductions, establishing their own niches. And reaping the rewards of high profit margins. Often it is the product development cycle that consumes the most time.

Analyzing the development process from project inception to customer delivery would reveal the big consumers of time. Action could then be taken to reduce, or eliminate whatever is possible. While doing so, it should be remembered that time spent on defining the product more completely saves time spent on making prototypes manufacturable. Technology has made available Rapid Prototyping and other visualization tools that help to save time, by making a greater number of design reiterations. This eliminates errors, as it conjures up 3D models as easily as 2D drawings. In addition to implementing such technologies, devising solid strategies like conducting bench marks and emulating the best in the field, would also help. PDM is another resource that organizes, manages and tracks information needs, making access valuable. The key for saving time would be in finding the right tools and using them effectively. The aim should be to establish a corporate culture conducive to cross functional team work and to get the employees to do their jobs more effectively.

Comparison of tasks with activities of the organization would disclose tasks not contributing to a desired activity. Activities must be examined periodically for their contribution to the performance of the organization's basic function.

On a lighter vein, the value of time can be realized by asking: the student who failed a grade (a year lost), mother who gave birth to a premature baby (a month earlier), a person who missed a train (for a minute), one who just avoided an accident (by a second) and an Olympic athlete who won a silver (because of a milli-second).

SUMMARY

A sound understanding of the concept of value can help to direct efforts towards the right kind of results to enhance value. It enables distinguishing between more or less, on the one hand, and better and worse, on the other. It helps the decision-maker to hit the golden mean. How critical it is to strike a balance, nobody questions. However, the fact remains that none knows how it is done. Moderate and persistent effort in the right direction has greater value than massive and periodic efforts in the wrong direction.

Here are some ground rules for enhancing value:

1. "Nothing can have value without being an object of utility," (Karl Marx).
2. Value is a relationship, established by comparison.
3. Use value and esteem value are related to the physical properties, features and attributes that make the product or service satisfy the customer. Cost and exchange value are related to the economic characteristics.
4. Value is utility measured against price, "the lowest cost to reliably provide the required function or service," (A.E. Mudge, 1989) or "the lowest cost at which a function, by any means, can be accomplished effectively, reliably and well."
5. A product or service with right attributes, features and function for the needs will be of value to the customer.
6. Value is directly related to function. The customer is especially interested in the function that satisfies the need.
7. Feasible attributes, features and functions are many. So also, the permutations and combinations, differentiation and costs. Value is in finding the point of balance, between needs (of the customer), offerings (of the company), and price (or costs). Just right, neither less, nor more.
8. When right is understood for a given purpose, the point of golden balance is struck between value and costs. "Anything more will be unnecessary and wasteful," (Tufty, 1983).

9. The value change of any enhancement will depend on its additional merit (use, performance, esteem, satisfaction, etc.) and the difference in cost.
10. Company performance, product performance and service are measured in terms of value added.
11. The value of a product or service depends on controllable internal factors. Here is scope for value enhancing effort.
12. Value comes from improved application.
13. Value also depends on applied situation, external to the company. Corollary: for each customer-product combination, there is a value chain of activities - another area for value enhancing efforts.
14. Value is the lowest cost at which a function, by any means, can be accomplished, effectively, reliably and well. Value enhancing here derives from improving the Primary Function and limiting the Secondary or Support Functions to inescapable minimum.
15. Customer value lies in his or her critical success factors. The best customer is the customer who cannot afford to do without your value and the contribution it makes to his or her functioning, growth and competitive advantage.
16. The customer redefines the value of a current product or service, when any company caters to a level of excellence, in any one component (attribute, feature or function), and sustains it.
17. Value means excellence all round - on performance, capability, features, attributes, quality, service, et al. At any point of time. No compromises.
18. Customer expectations of value change and escalate fast.
19. The goal is create, build or add value by:
    - designing value (with creativity, superior ideas, material, methods and process);
    - producing value (with technology, equipment, skill, innovation and workmanship);
    - supplying value (performance, use, esteem, satisfaction and returns);
    - assuring value (backing with warranty and efficient service); and
    - delivering the highest value to the customer or user.

Reasons for Poor Value

- Lack of Information
- Lack of Ideas
- Lack of Time
- Lack of Attention
- Lack of Listening
- Lack of Problem Ownership
- Poor Quality
- Honest Wrong Beliefs
- Habitual Thinking
- Risk of Personal Loss
- Reluctance to Seek Advice
- Habits and Attitudes
- Unrealistic Requirements
- Temporary or Changed Circumstances
- Changing Technology
- Poor Communications
- Prejudice
- Misconceptions
- Lack of Experience
- Desire to Conform
- Poor Interaction among Contributing Disciplines
- Comfortable High Cost Activities
- Creep
- Non-value-Adding Work
- Waste
- Shape a Winner

4 REASONS FOR POOR VALUE

Poor value is really a people problem. Reasons for poor value are many. The major contributors are as follows.

LACK OF INFORMATION

Information, correctly used, is power. That is why today people go to information, rather than information coming to them. With the right information one can do almost anything.

Lack of information (and right information) can be due to:

- Failure to get sufficient relevant facts.
- Lack of knowledge or misunderstanding of the full requirements.
- Non-availability of full information.
- Non-transmittal of information in suitable form.
- Misinterpretation of available information.
- Inaccurate definition of the problem or the project itself.
- Limited information.
- System bias, channelling information narrowly.

Information that is most frequently lacking is technical information on changes, to keep up with the technological explosion; and cost information on comparable costs of various solutions to a given problem. Usually, these are neither compiled, nor up-dated; and, when done, not in a form that would help decision-making. Especially, when new processes, materials and methods are tried for the first time. Because new products, new processes and new materials are constantly entering the market, it becomes a difficult task to remain knowledgeable on all changes. To investigate a number of different processes or materials, to look for standard parts, to compare costs, etc. need time (refer item 3, following), the lack of which breeds unnecessary costs. "Lack of information and the relative cost" thereof in these cases is estimated to "add something like 25 percent to the cost of a component," (Raven, 1971).

One of the early jobs that Miles had undertaken was the value study of the Westinghouse Hot Point Refrigerator. On its thermostat control, the wire clip to hold the cover was made of phosphor bronze. It cost $ 7,000 a year. The designer had specified the best material for the part - non-ferrous to prevent corrosion; and flexing without breakage, to allow repeated opening and closing. Had he the information that the clip needed to flex only an average 6 times in its life, he would not have specified for this component *phosphor bronze with its characteristic of flexing ten to hundred thousand times before breakage.* By changing to spring brass, the same job could be done for $ 3,000 a year (Miles, 1972).

Competition is a fact of life. Deregulation, globalisation of trade and adoption of international standards opened unlimited opportunities for business and industries. They are now able to produce a variety of goods and services, with little to differentiate between them. That has shrunk today's competitive advantage to matters of knowledge and skill. For, it has become necessary not merely to find, but also invent, new competitive advantages. Therefore, knowing the competition is just as important as knowing the customer, or your product or service. Immediate competitor, distant competitor, current competitor, and potential competitor, others in the same line of business, any business whatsoever: there is no end to the coverage needed for information. A steel plant has to worry about not only other steel plants, but also aluminium plants, engineered plastics, etc. The need is to know not only others strengths and weaknesses, but more importantly, their objectives in technology leadership, strategies in costs, and response patterns. The goal is for one to deliver extraordinary levels of distinctive value, and more of it, as compared to the competitors.

The best way is to gather what information can be got and then act, or plan the action required. Telecommunications, micro electronics, fibre optics and information highways are being used in creative ways, to bring information age capabilities to every one. It is possible now to simultaneously transmit voice, data, video and graphics over a single copper telephone wire and over fibre optic cable.

Thomas Friedman writes in his book "The word is Flat", page 8, that *it is now possible for more people than ever to collaborate and compete in real time with more other people on more different kinds of work from more different corners of the planet and on more equal footing than at any time in the history of the world."*

Vital information to modify the product or service to suit the customer comes from interaction among internal functions, external suppliers, distributors, and customers themselves.

Customers are on the move too. Their needs and tastes are changing. They seek greater variety and quality, durability, convenience and customised alternatives with special features suiting individual requirements. To remain responsive to their changing needs, to add customer friendly features, widespread availability of information is necessary. For effective, day-to-day, problem-solving, visual display of information speeds up dissemination and spurs actions.

Knowing how to focus or re-focus information to improve performance is equally important. Few companies do. Too often their Managers are mired in the complexity of their tasks. They believe that every employee understands the basic building blocks of how their business works. Most do. However, many do not. They do not realize how important the fundamentals - cash, margin, velocity, improvement and growth – are. Unless, of course, the Manager explains them, in the context of the entire business - and, often. This is a cost-free opportunity for prospering, especially when the economy is in the doldrums.

To quote a Nigerian proverb, "not knowing is bad; not wanting to know is worse." How true !

LACK OF IDEAS

Reason, scant use and application of knowledge and skills, available in the organisation, outside the organisation, in standards, or with specialists and professional forums.

Any one can generate ideas. 3M developed a sand paper that could be used wet, when their sales representatives saw workers in automobile plants choking with the dust produced while dry sanding. 3M also came up with disposable surgical staples and seri-strip for closing incisions, by observing problems in hospital operating rooms.

Nobody is perfect and so, no one person can think of everything. This makes creative ideas a rarity. There was only one Ted Turner, who utilised Oatville Communications to create CNN; one Bill Gates, who applied operating software for personal computers; and one Howard Head, who innovated metal skis and over-sized tennis rackets; one Edwin Land, who pioneered instant photography. Nicholas Hayack, the man who put millions of Swatches on the wrists all over the world, has now created a Swatch Mobile, the MCC Smart. This teeny-weeny small car is a two-seater. It is 10 percent smaller than a typical sub-compact. Its 600 cc turbo charged engine weighs a tenth of any existing engine with equal power.

Ideas are free; but, key to success. General Electric's Jack Welch redeemed the company in the red to profitability with his ideas of *boundary-less-ness, speed and stretch. By Boundary-lessness* he meant that an idea could be from any source, so search the globe for ideas. *Speed* meant that it is better to act quickly than waiting too long for right answers and loose the opportunity. With *stretch*, he wanted to energise the organisation to pursue big dreams and not just remain comfortable doing routine business. Yokogawa of Japan used *bullet train thinking.* Bob Gavin of Motorola stressed *quantum leap* for improving quality by a factor of 10. Gillette Company sought to *earn more from each customer.* Gillette continually upgraded customers worldwide from inexpensive disposable and double edge razors to technically superior products that justify a premium, like Mach 3. Henry Ford built his auto empire with efficient production of an *acceptable product at the lowest price* possible. 3M and Hewlett-Packard established completely new markets with *break-through products and extensions* (Post it Notes, Ink Jet technology, PC industry). Nucor, maker of steel and steel products, Dell Computer Corp., Maytag Corp., and Wal-Mart Stores Inc., went in for *operational excellence,* selecting what they do best and delivering it to the customers. They strove to provide value as perceived by the customer: *lowest total cost.* Intel and Nike pushed performance boundaries to gain and sustain *product leadership.* Airborne Express cultivated relationships for unique needs, becoming *customer friendly* (Treacy, M. 1995), providing the best solution for them. Ameritech Corp. used *customer intimacy* (Treacy, M. 1995), focusing not on what the market wants, but what specific customers want. They pinpointed specific customer segments (like banks, airlines, small businesses, work-at-home customers, Government, etc.) and tailored business services to match their specific needs. The idea of Harley Davidson is not only to make and sell motor cycles, but also to create and own a *customer life style.* Kazuo Inamori's management philosophy–*the amoebae system* - breaks down the divisions of Kyocera Corp. and its affiliates into smallest business units with its own profit and loss responsibility. This idea has made his company the world leader, and him, the Japanese entrepreneur extraordinary. Staples applied the *super market model* to office supplies, office electronics and office furniture. Siemens A.G. is revitalising its global structure with *TOP,* a corporate program that is *improving the way it delivers technological solutions to customers* through innovation and growth. In the last 20 years. Japan cut energy cost of their finished products by 60 percent. They achieved this by pushing *investment in energy efficient technology.* If they do not have a technology, they buy it form the best source. If they cannot innovate very well, they make the Universities do it for them, by endowing professorships. Japanese companies insist on adding value (zo-shu zo-eki, meaning increased sales and operating margins) or use OMMIT guide that defines Objectives, identifies Market opportunities, understand Money and its use as company resource, uses good Information systems in support and Team approach to management. *Service with soul,* is an idea to take an extra step or steps to please and delight the customer. That is what NYPRO, an injection molder, did. They got rid of 90 percent of their customers, so that they could *focus extravagant* (and profitable) *service* on the remaining 10 percent. They built a plant next to one customer without the customer even guaranteeing them a long term contract. The result; turning an ordinary commodity - injection molded plastics - into an extraordinary service.

Conventional target setting examples are a prescribed increase in productivity (say +10 percent), a lowering of expense budget (say 20 percent cut), a harsher limit on resource holding (say 50 percent reduction in inventory) and so on. These are seen as *threatening goals.*

A creative version of goals would be *tough stretch goals,* such as an improvement in cycle time (reduction by 25 percent), a betterment of assembly time (improvement by 50 percent), reduction in scrap and re-work (say 40 percent), and such like.

Yet another deficiency is in the way ideas are implemented. Every 4 to 5 years, companies try to introduce a product variation or a new generation of products. The conventional focus goes to maximising current functions - particularly, efficiencies, yields, bringing down cost of variety, and the like. Other ideas are side tracked.

LACK OF TIME

Another component of value is time. Time is truly money and one of the best ways to save money is to save time. Time waste is most difficult to identity and isolate, as it does not litter the floor. Lack of time is most common and universal.

When a project is finally approved, there is pressure to provide it as quickly as possible. Time pressure is so great that the Designer's prime objective becomes getting a solution off the board within the allotted time. Time is not available to make every study or comparison desired. His decision-making works on the principle of what Simon calls satisficing, the search stopping when coming across the first solution that is good enough. There is little or no effort to consider properly, if at all, the value of the design approach being developed. Or, to optimise the many solutions to a given design, based on cost, or to comb through and develop fully even the one in hand. Seldom is there time to sit back and contemplate ideas, or to design or to develop alternative approaches or solutions. The design proposed is more likely to be either a scaled up or scaled down version of a successful predecessor. Naturally, it will include the faults and deficiencies of the previous design; difficulties of manufacture, assembly, servicing, testing and inspection; high scrap rate; wrong choice of materials; and so on.

Dead lines are helpful to complete the job in time. However, they generally do not permit complete searching, testing, and seeing and utilising information which would otherwise have enabled accomplishing customer needs at the lowest cost - be it in design, engineering, purchasing or manufacturing. Inertia prompts choosing a rather traditional fastening, finish, fit or tolerance - rather than checking it for appropriateness, before specifying. *"Lack of time aspect of unnecessary cost could add up to 15 percent or more of the ex-works cost of a product."* (Raven, 1971).

The message is on the time spent. The time one spends on every item is a measure of the intensity, priority and concern for the item. What you spend your time on becomes the organisation's preoccupation (see also item 4, Lack of Attention). Each day has a defined capacity. One has to estimate and calculate how long it takes to do the task and then evaluate whether the available time is enough to do them. There will be need to sort the tasks, purge some, assign slots for the tasks to be done, containerise them within the time allotted and equalise. It will need investment in time and effort to successfully manage time. Focussing on the bigger picture of goals will help in accomplishing the most in the time available.

Turn travel time to productive time.

Technological advances have re-priced the value of time and reset customers' expectations. Conventional tools are much too slow for today's needs. Just-In-Time technique, linked backward to the supplier and forward, to the customer and Electronic Data Interchange, reduce lead times, inventory, and costs; raises service level and accuracy in ordering, shipping and receiving; and minimize out of stock situations.

Speed of response is an essential value dimension. Sony, JVC and Phillips raced to perfect their individual VCR technology. However, Phillips V 2000, launched in Europe some 18 months after JVC's VHS, was dead on arrival. JVC had sold several million VCRs round the world and so could excel: even add cost reduction and feature improvements to keep on winning.

In the Sixties, Tata Steel wanted to double its production capacity to 2 million tonnes of ingot steel per year, making the changes and additions without interfering with production. A project of such magnitude and complexity would normally need 5 years, design to full commissioning. Tatas attempted to compress the time to 30 months, causing costs to double; and besides, suffered innumerable start-up and running-in problems, as well as substantial loss of production.

LACK OF ATTENTION

The conventional approach is to accept that a certain amount of error is normal. For instance, you expect the plane or train to be late; the mail to go astray and not get delivered; the equipment would breakdown; etc. You expect things to go wrong all the time. This is all right for planning and estimating; but not for execution. Whereas, by paying serious attention to every detail, you can be prepared for exigency, even for the most unlikely events. It is obsessive; but, at the final reckoning, you would be a winner, having thought of everything and being in complete control.

At Tokyo Railway Station, you can stand at a marked spot on the platform and when the train arrives, the doors will open right in front of you. Trains are on time. Bags are not lost. Connections are not missed. Here every thing works, as the Japanese have paid, and continue to pay, attention to precision and detail. The clothier, Lands' End, remembers your last order, your family members' sizes, etc.

TV, riches to rags saga in USA, is another classic, but different type of example. There was a time when every TV manufacturer was US based. Every job for TV, from Research and Development and Design through manufacturing and marketing, was American. Nevertheless, no more. Reason: they targeted only American customers, offered others the same products designed for American customers, and failed to devote attention to modify the product and match the specific needs of overseas customers. To the list can be added left-hand drive cars, huge refrigerators, items made to BSS, etc.

Conventional management routine includes spending time to check and control production plans, schedules and progress, maintenance and service, cost, and such like items. However, the agenda for none of the meetings, at plant level, management level or board level, include checks and controls on the *value* of the product or service. Only revising the priorities can solve this lack of attention: showing that value is what the management is most concerned about. The message is on time spent (see also item 3, Lack of Time).

LACK OF LISTENING

Listening, like many things simple, is not so simple. It has five main objectives:

- as a means to gather information and applicable ideas;
- to keep in touch with several sources - employees, suppliers, distributors, customers, etc.;
- to collect quickly all information, especially on things concerning the product or service that trouble the customers;
- to motivate everyone in the organisation to correlate the information gathered with result-oriented opportunities;
- to share, and disseminate widely, ideas and information.

Effective listening is engaged listening. It means paying attention. The best way to do so is to use all listening techniques - listening systematically, listening carefully, listening for facts, listening for perceptions, listening naively, and so on.

Many do not listen. On the other hand, what starts out as listening often deteriorates to getting in touch with; then, making others understand; and ends up, talking, telling and educating. The fact is you never learn anything talking.

The more closely you looked, you will see more examples of senior executives failing to listen to their middle managers. Middle Managers are close to day to day operations, customers and front line employees. They are more diverse in functional area, work experience, geography, gender and ethnic background. Thus, they are fertile ground for creative ideas. However, for want of listening, good ideas routinely die before they even see the light of the day.

In listening studies, women used both the left (analytical) and right (feeling) sides of the brain. Men used the left side of the brain. Managing for value encourages use of both sides of the brain - the right, for blasting creative ideas and the left, for later judicial analysis.

Many simply assume that they know better than the customers, co-workers, etc. Whereas, most ideas are rooted in workers' practical needs, or in the minds of service people and customers, waiting for someone to listen. Most unsuccessful products are not technically deficient, but have too much technology, at far too high a price. It is common to consider feed back from customers, service people and sales as wish lists to make their lives easier. Functional barriers are too many. Successful companies had better, faster, inter-actions that create, make and market values.

Both Tom Peters, with his idea of "managing by walking round" and Rene McPherson, with his emphasis on "managing from the bottom up" base their approaches on true listening.

Melville Shoe, a small, undistinguished shoe chain of 1960s, became one of the fastest growing and most profitable fashion retailers in America, listening to customers and exploring their values.

LACK OF PROBLEM OWNERSHIP

The lack of problem ownership, particularly where job specialisation is strict and severe, causes many problems (solvable in a very simple way) to stay unresolved. Often in situations, the employee would say, it is not his or her problem; let the other person fix it. In many cases, he or she would say what is being done wrong; he or she could show how to do it right. His or her excuse for not doing right himself or herself is that he or she would neither get credit; nor any monetary benefit; nor recognition.

An example from auto air conditioning. They should not be too noisy, as, otherwise, it would mar listening to the stereo. Quick cooling would require high-speed blowers. If the blower is too noisy, the Air conditioning Technician cannot say, "it is not my problem. I only want to cool the car." Similarly, the Audio Technician cannot say, "it is not my problem, my units are ok." Both have to look at the problem as the total system of the car and set it right.

Group Technology, practised by some industries, has tried to overcome this problem. Each group completes all the tasks required to complete an item.

Semco, Brazil, is considered the best plant in that country. It is run on participatory management principles and profits are shared with the workers. They have no job descriptions. The shop floor level personnel are either Associates or Coordinators. Associates do research, design, sales and manufacturing. Coordinators lead teams and tasks. Most people can do several jobs. They take on more and more tasks, as needed - security, cleaning, driving vehicles, cooking food in the canteens, etc.

POOR QUALITY

Everyone is for quality. But, what they usually have in mind is a product or service free of defects. This is a narrow view and quite dangerous in today's market place. The world class concept of quality, involves perfecting the process, rather than weeding out the defectives. It also means that the product or service is produced quickly and with the features and benefits that the customer wants. There should be as little waste as possible. It should also be at a price that is fair, delivered when the customer wants it and with excellent follow-up provisions.

Quality has always been a criterion for value - be it in Defence, consumer products, or service. If people are not in the quality process today, they may not be in business in the future. Determining what the customers want is not as easy as it might sound. Besides, until recently, customers lacked the means to objectively evaluate product performance. Conditions have changed. Now, manufactures have to contend with better-educated customers and consumer advocates or protection groups, who assess global markets and rate quality by relative comparison.

Early practitioners of quality methods used specifications and standards to inspect and accept the quality of the products. Conformance was the criterion. These specifications and standards were based on internally generated measures and comparisons. So much so, when companies spend heavily on feature, it meant little to the customers, or added to the price of the product without perceived benefits (or value).

Without quality, there is no value. Quality adds value at each step of the product creation. It is something that has to be measured at the customers' end and not in the manufacturing plants. Quality is integrity to the manufacturing system. Quality has to be built during the production phase. Quality is not just eliminating what is not good. Many characteristics of unacceptable quality in manufacture are traceable to the absence of such an approach in design and in management of the business process. The least cost remedy lies before the fact, during design. However, it can also be had after the fact, during manufacture and service, though to a lesser degree of return.

Quality does not mean quality of the product and service alone. It means *total quality.* That is, it includes such items as quality reliability, quality of communication, quality of relationships, quality of guarantees, etc. Conformance to specifications is only the beginning. The concept has progressed from "fitness to specification" to "fitness to need," and currently, "fitness to latent need," *i.e.,* what the customers might truly value, but have never experienced, or would never think to ask for. The real test of quality will be how the customer perceives the specifications and what it means to him to work with products and services conforming to those specifications. If there are no complaints on quality from the customers, it may not prove that the quality offered is the best. It might reflect customer apathy - living with the quality problems created by the product or service, and not complaining. Interaction with the customer will open out wide vista of quality improvements that are possible and desirable. More often than not, it will be seen that value can be added through appropriate, but small changes or improvements, most of which could be costing little money; but many such. *Kaizen,* as the Japanese say – and not Kayo. Kaizen is a Japanese word, meaning *constant and never ending improvement.* It is a process of observation and deliberate, patient, continual, incremental refinements of current products, processes and methods. Each time, the products get a little better, a little smaller, less costly and more customer-friendly. Copeland Corporation's Scroll Compressor plant had, in the last 18 months, instituted 42 Kaizen quick step improvement projects, to gain $ 2 million by way of reduced operating costs.

The Japanese firms' view of total quality and serving the customer is an evolution over several years. They demonstrate their quality ethics everywhere, even in such simple items as a tooth pick. Their toothpick is a work of art, perfectly round, with a sculptured end; and all, with exactly the same dimensions. Other commercial counterparts are splinters of wood in a box.

Quality is capital-intensive. IBM says the cost of poor quality runs from 15 percent to 40 percent of gross resources, depending on the maturity of the products. Tom Peters says it absorbs 25 percent of all the people and all the assets of a manufacturing company to do the re-work and other tasks caused by poor quality; and in service, 40 percent. To improve quality, while at the same time cutting costs, is a big headache that few executives only find systematic methods to solve. Virtually, every product Rubber Maid makes is a smash hit, as it has always been a quality house. To them cost reduction is just poker stakes; and innovation is the critical driver. The American Auto industry is reported to be now on the verge of an affordability crisis or, at least, a value crisis. The Japanese seem to have forced the quality level of all vehicles of all producers to rise. Cars are lasting longer, they are much safer, and they have more optional accessories. But, the higher quality, safety and extras have not come free. The labour and engineering costs are higher. None the less, these advances are expected to continue. But, the customers are smart. One who could buy a car 20 years ago for about 26.5 weeks' family income. Now it needs 30.6 weeks income to buy the latest model. That, the consumers are unwilling to pay, as the trend of recent sales decline forewarns. They now want value for their money!

Most companies are catching up with each other in quality, to meet the easing of trade barriers and the passing of ISO Standards. Soon quality will cease to be a meaningful criterion to differentiate between products or suppliers. However, quality per cost will continue to be a major determinant.

HONEST WRONG BELIEFS

Some decisions are based on erroneous beliefs, rather than on facts. A situation is often assumed to be impossible, for erroneous, but sincere reasons. For example, Planners who make decisions on what a project should accomplish may not have properly gauged the public's needs. Designers who make decisions on what material, process, fastener or factor of safety to use, may be biased against some specific items, because of one or more unfortunate experiences of failure (personal or hearsay). Examples of design decisions based on wrong beliefs are:

- Spheroidal graphitic iron was once considered too brittle.
- Electric overhead travelling crane gear breakage was attributed to poor hardness of gear teeth. To correct, oil quenching was replaced by flame hardening. Gear hardness increased; so also the breakages, as the better hardening process also increased the brittleness.
- Down time for replacement of fast-wearing slurry transfer pumps was said to be due to poor quality of material in the pump parts; whereas, it was the linear speed of flow that caused the rapid wear. Lowering the speed virtually eliminated down time for replacements of worn out parts, during production runs. It also enabled moving greater volume of slurry.

- Plastics were considered brittle and weak. Once they were. No longer.
- Sheet steel was most economical for thin enclosures. That was until vacuum die casting and high strength plastic molding became available.

Half-truths compound the problem.

A sound improvement could be abandoned, because it was thought it might cost too much. An equally sound reduction in cost could be turned down because it was thought it could hurt performance. Product worth is improved in the sincere belief that the added cost would be reasonable. And, the product cost is reduced with the fervent hope that the reduction would not lower the product worth. These are daily occurrences.

Traditional accounting reports - on cost, cost variance, productivity, efficiency, output, sales, market share, and profit and loss - are expected to highlight good work, thus motivating in the right direction. The trouble is that these accounting reports are retrospective measures, made much after real events. Therefore, their timing usually misfires leading to making wrong decisions - admonishing good performance, rewarding wrong work unit, and passing out blame or praise in one period for what people did in a previous one. Some accounting practices also do not reflect values - deferred charges, last minute inventory re-evaluations, earnings, management practices, excessive write downs which are later reversed, etc.

General Motors prided themselves to be the Number One automakers in the world, until 1980, when the Japanese entered the market with their hot selling Toyota. GM honestly wrongly thought Japanese had an edge over the Americans because of lower labour costs. They calculated that producing millions of units on highly automated plants, with robots for every conceivable operation, would lower American labour costs to the barest minimum. They envisaged flooding the market with a standard quality product and regaining their lost ranking. GM honestly wrongly believed that with the massive investment of $ 70 billion in technology for their Hamtrack assembly plant. everything would work. It did not. What started out as a technocrat's dream turned into a management nightmare. Robots painted each other, instead of cars. Expensive automated vehicles sat idle, while computer programmers tried to get the lines moving.

Encyclopaedia Britannica, the 225-year-old publisher, honestly wrongly believed that they could continue to reign supreme because of the rich and vast knowledge content of their tomes. They continued with direct sales of their world famous multi-volume books. In 1995, they became almost bankrupt, when Comptons, Groliers and Encarta, started selling their not so good encyclopaedias on CD-ROMs. Customers preferred the space saving units, purchasable from direct mail catalogues and computer stores.

Xerox honestly wrongly believed that customers would not want small desktop copiers.

The US Television industry wrongly thought that the customers would not want colour portables.

Harley Davidson wrongly believed that there would be no great demand for small motor cycles. Honda stole the market.

Recor wrongly believed that japanese women would continue to use sewn clothing when readymades were flooding the markets. They wrongly believed that perfecting their sewing machines would be the answer to maintain their market share.

HABITUAL THINKING

Thinking and doing things in the same way is a frequent cause of poor value. However, it is extremely difficult to undo the things one has been doing for years.

It is a habit to judge people by what you have become used to in your environment. Like, wearing casual clothes is construed as not taking the business seriously. Nodding during the meeting is taken as understanding. A foreigner good at English is said to be good at everything else; and, one with difficulty in communicating, not good at his job. If one uses different tenses or voice for consecutive sentences, it is thought that the speaker is hiding or falsifying something.

An average specialist in industry thinks only in terms of a limited range of materials, methods, processes, etc. A man who has been brought up to "think steel" will do so: a plastics man will "think plastics."

Most people have a habit of re-using what worked the last time or copying a standard set by others. They duplicate a success, repeat a good experience and avoid a bad one. This is a defensive measure, to minimise risks, and is prevalent because of rigid use of standard designs, rules and procedures, customs, traditions, etc.

The habit of perfecting the product to beat competition and maintain market share made Recor, a Japanese Sewing Machine maker, to concentrate on perfecting its product. However, in the meantime, Japanese women switched from sewn clothing to ready-mades. Recor went soon out of business, although their product was very good.

General Motors clung to its belief that its dominant design (front engine, full sized rear wheel drive, and chassis mounting) was invulnerable to any threat. They did not pursue their compact car initiative. Its market share declined to 38 percent.

Often, yesterday's good ideas become today's policy guidelines and tomorrow's rules and regulations.

Almost invariably, every error leads to an investigation and pinning the blame on some one. What is unfortunate is the preoccupation with fixing the blame - and not fixing the problem. What is more important, and value adding, is to know what exactly had gone wrong and how to remedy it.

In the Fifties, America was the world's leading manufacturer of TV sets. 27 American companies, like Zenith, RCA, GE and Emerson had a solid technological lead over foreign manufacturers. American companies were successful around the world, except Japan. To sell in Japan, the only option open was to license their technology to Japanese companies. Consequently, Japan got American technology for own use. Soon, Japan began to make cheap black and white TVs and exported them to America. By 1976, the entire American black and white sales were imports. America did not make these any more. American companies moved to colour and, again, licensed colour technology to Japan. But, the Japanese also started an intensive program to develop colour TV s, and making it in their protected markets, flooded American markets with exports. By 1987, only one American company, Zenith, was making colour TV s. Licensing had become so much of a habit with America that, again, when Ampex, the California firm, invented the VCR in 1959, America did not even try to make a commercial product. They rushed to license the technology to Japan and moved on. That is how Japan now reigns supreme in TV-VCR business.

RISK OF PERSONAL LOSS

Any good Engineer or Manager knows that nothing is *for sure.* But, they also know that anything that is done over and over again has less possibility of failures as compared to something new and unknown. Failure of a new approach could cause a personal loss of face to the suggestor and/or decision-maker. People fear the consequent ridicule or humiliation.

Fear is a conditioned response, a life sucking habit that can easily consume one's energy and creativity, if one is not careful. It is one's own creation. Therefore, it should be as easy to tear it down as it is to feel it.

The British researcher, Malcolm Trevor summarises in "The Japanese Management System," that British managers view sharing information as a danger to their own career prospects. Productivity enhancing computers were resisted because it would decrease the number of personnel reporting to the boss; and, in turn, would reduce his status and salary. Such fears are a common human tendency.

In the Sixties, RCA Laboratories worked on solving various problems associated with Liquid-Crystal-Display (LCD) technology. They even created various prototype devices that showed the potential of this break through technology. However, because some managers saw LCDs as a threat to their status quo, RCA was unable to transfer a technology success into a business success. The Japanese did.

Fear of risk of personal loss, ridicule or humiliation kills creativity and innovation.

When, in manufacturing, an engineer spends weeks perfecting an assembly line or a processing technique; or a designer designs a part or a product; or a buyer decides on a purchase: they feel that they have put something into it. They resent changes. To them, no pain is as great as the pain of change. Perhaps, it is the natural fear of the unknown: but, more often than not, the point is over stretched for the slightest excuse. Some others feel that they, and only they, always provide for the best in their approaches. Over the years, this feeling cumulates to form a negative attitude of resistance to change.

RELUCTANCE TO SEEK ADVICE

Designers and Planners are renown for their reluctance to seek advice from others, and to admit that they do not know the answer. Architects, Planners and Engineers should seek advice of competent experts if maximum design value is to be achieved, with the information explosion reaching today unprecedented heights.

This is said of Japan. A century ago, Japan was a feudal society. The Japanese realised that they had to change, if only to continue to prosper. The Meiji revolution opened Japan to the world. Starting in the 1860s, they brought in thousands of Western specialists to advise them on how to change their government and their industries. The entire society underwent a revolution. After the Second World War, this was repeated, particularly in commerce and industry, with equally dramatic results. Time was, when Japanese goods were synonymous with rotten quality. In 1950, they asked Dr. Deming to help them to improve the quality of their products. Then, Prof. Juran. They asked Miles to help them with Value Engineering, in 1960. In fact, as tributes for their assistance, the Japanese have instituted some best performance awards for industries and Value Specialists: the Deming Prize and Miles VE Awards. Thus today, Japan has transformed itself into a formidable world class business competitor in field after field.

Malaysia is the largest producer of palm oil, but it was all being processed abroad. That was until, after she attained Independence, United Plantations of Malaysia invited Tata Oil Mills, India, to provide expert advice for the management of the world's largest and most integrated palm oil processing plant. Thus was born Unitata.

Success of Korea and Taiwan are classic examples of what seeking advice can beget.

HABITS AND ATTITUDES

"The deepest law of human nature is habit," wrote Carlyle. It "works more constantly and with greater force than reason." "Which (reason) is seldom fairly consulted and more rarely, obeyed," remarks Locke. How true!

Often the force of habit results in developing a pattern of thinking, of doing things, of solving problems, and so on. Habit solutions are often obsolete solutions. No doubt, the advantages gained are speedier preparation of drawings and easier meeting of time schedules. However, the disadvantages do not become apparent immediately. For, the unnecessary cost that the habit solution breeds does not manifest until much later and is, often, unknown to the Designer.

Some specialists tend to feel that their specialised knowledge is their security. Some others have the ostrich attitude that what they do know, or will not allow others to know, will protect them from change. Still others have a false sense of pride, which keeps them from consulting others. This is a real life situation and mars professional leadership.

Traditions and habits are hard to break. Habits are what we use to build basic skills; and so, many are beneficial. Like excellence, which, according to Aristotle, "is not an art, but a habit." Habits supported by attitudes and becoming roadblocks are disadvantageous. Unquestioned conventions and unchallenged precedents get entrenched as managerial habits. Many decisions are based on long established habits built on company procedures, methods, tooling concepts, supplier relationships, etc.

Attitude is a matter of choice. A positive attitude begets positive results and a habit of searching for alternatives and possibilities. A negative attitude, on the other hand, begets negative results and a habit of blocking alternatives. An attitude of indifference produces indifferent results. Records are set and broken by men, when one believes in oneself and believes that there is nothing that is impossible to achieve, given the necessary effort, time and resources.

Attitudes have a big influence in decision making. They are tough and difficult to change. During the progression in life, we develop an attitude screen. At birth our attitude screens are clear. But, as years go by, clouds begin to develop within the attitude screen, tempered by experience. Chances are that, when confronted with enigmas, paradoxes, puzzles, riddles and mysteries of the market place, the clouds tend to become thicker and denser.

Some people become reluctant to change of any kind and regardless of the merits of the proposal. This is true, especially, if the change directly affects their plans, or design, or jobs.

In talent-intensive business, such as high technology, entertainment, and some financial services, an attitude is prevalent that the success of the business depends on the unique expertise of the top man. In European companies, there is an attitude of "I know best." Often these are smoke screens for an unwillingness to change.

Charles Kittering once stated that nine hundred and ninety nine people out of a thousand, when presented with a new idea, would immediately give the proposer all reasons why it would not work. The sole exception will give reasons why he thinks it would work.

It is truly said that "habits" take us where we were yesterday and our "attitudes" keep us there.

UNREALISTIC REQUIREMENTS

Requirements are often unrealistically specified or grossly over stated with reference to performance, materials, safety, procedures, fits, tolerances and finishes. That is because people like to play safe. Sometimes requirements are assumed (by the Planner or Designer), when none are specifically indicated. Traditionally, Designers concentrate on development of a reliable system that exceeds all known and assumed requirements. The net result is over-design, with attendant excess cost. Requirements are not usually challenged to determine actual needs.

"The Relative Costs of Finishes and Tolerances," a bulletin published by Tapco Group of Thompson Ramo Wooldridge, show some interesting data:

- Cost of surface roughness multiplies four times per step from 125 micro inch to 32; and 32 to 8.
- Cost of tolerance becomes double from 0.040 to 0.010; five times more from 0.020 to 0.002; and exponential below 0.001.
- Cost of drilled hole increases with depth.
- Cost of shafting increases as tolerances tighten and length increases.
- Having ten points difference in Rockwell "C" hardness scale makes a big dent in the costs.

For the Mon Fayette Expressway in Pennsylvania State, USA, the authorities wanted to use their favoured design of H piles for the bridge across one large creek. Calculations showed that it would necessitate H x 14 x 73 Ibs. piles; boring 20 ft diameter bore holes; and quite a lot of cement and filling. It looked unrealistic. On re-examination, it was possible to substitute 9 thick-walled piping, which needed smaller bore holes and lesser filling. The saving was $ 2 million.

For the Skelp Mill in Tata Steel, the bearings required *mirror finish.* So, the spares used to be imported from the suppliers, incurring heavy cost and scarce foreign exchange. During the drive for import substitution and conservation of foreign exchange, this was one of the many items for which Sources Development Department was finding local sources. None had equipment to supply mirror finish; but one supplier, offered a fine finish substitute bearing that was manufacturable with his limited facilities. It was scheduled to be tried in the Mill, by replacing the worn out imported bearing during an annual shut down. Unfortunately, the change over was missed. The substitute bearing lay at site, acquiring a fine coating of rust, while waiting for reschedule of the change. When making the change the foreman was hesitant to use the substitute bearing with its fine coat of rust. Hence, it was sent to the Shops, where it was given a fine cut before the change. The Mill operated well with the substitute bearing. It showed that *mirror finish* specified by the supplier could not be a technical necessity, but an *unrealistic requirement* - revealed only by an accident of circumstances and by action for unconnected purpose, and by unconnected agencies.

TEMPORARY OR CHANGED CIRCUMSTANCES

When pressed for a decision, we take to a temporary expedient, fondly hoping to get back to it later and make a review or correction. Only, this getting back to it seldom happens. For example, in a Steel Mill, the electric overhead travelling crane is the principal material handling equipment and critical for production. A broken down crane is quickly given back in service, shorting a relay, to avoid the down time and production loss that replacing it would entail, especially when the mill is on a production drive. The crane would continue to be in operation for a long time thereafter without scheduling a shut down to effect the replacement. Similarly, a cable fault is solved by drawing in parallel a temporary line. The likelihood is that the temporary line stays permanent.

A customer may no longer require all the features of the product originally specified. Certain operations, finishes, or tolerances may have been added to correct a temporary situation or an emergency. The emergency or situation may have disappeared or eased; but the operations are continued. For example, a forging may have been specified for a shaft, which necessitates certain amount of machining to finish. With the technological development in rolling practices, it could have been changed to rolled round: but, missed as for as correcting the part drawing or specification is concerned. Result: continued procurement of the shaft made from rolled round, but at cost including surface machining. Or, in an emergency, to offset die wear, certain machining operations could have been specified to remove excess material and to maintain surface finish. Even after change of die, the machining could continue in the specifications, unaltered.

The areas of unnecessary costs caused by temporary circumstances are painfully obvious, but only after they are revealed!

It is surprising how difficult it is to discern these situations from an apparently innocent looking piece of equipment, part, drawing, or specifications. Under normal conditions, intimate knowledge should help in finding its flaws and tracing the sources of problems. However, paradoxically, one, very familiar with the item, would not be able to detach oneself from the problem, to discover these inconsistencies, or to think about the item in new and imaginative ways. Insiders often confuse what is with what should be. Especially, if the organisation is old, large, well managed by bureaucratic procedures and successful in the past.

Beware of temporary solutions; they tend to become permanent.

CHANGING TECHNOLOGY

Once every century or so, the way of making things change with a sweeping flourish. Development of processes, products and materials makes available constantly changing, and many times lower cost, ways of performing the necessary functions. Right now, the world is on the verge of yet another addition to the list of developments. It should be no surprise then that an individual finds it difficult to keep up, be completely current, even in his own field of specialisation.

When a revolutionary new technology arrives, it will be wise to scrap the old. From vacuum tubes to semi conductors, technological transition led to disappearance of individual product lines and closure of many industries. Japanese companies profited by going from germanium to silicon, transistors to integrated circuits, analog to digital and circuits to microprocessors. Celanese beat Du Pont when polyester started replacing nylon bais-ply tire cords. Michelin beat Goodrich when the bias-ply again changed to the radial.

If wholesale change of technology were not possible, at least, when the outer performance limits of a successful product have been reached, it should be abandoned. Continuance beyond and trying to produce "one more generation" would be disastrous, as examples prove. Lockheed tried to coax one more generation out of piston aircraft, while Boeing was rendering obsolete piston technology with jets. Baldwin tried to extract one more generation out of steam locomotives, while General Electric was rendering obsolete steam technology with electric engines.

Tata Steel tried to squeeze one more generation out of Acid Bessemer Converters, while steel makers in Germany, Japan and Austria were rendering it obsolete and replacing it with L D process. NCR tried to refine its mechanical cash register to electro-mechanical design, when electronic machines were coming into the market. Vacuum tube makers persisted with their product lines and did not enter the solid state business. Wisdom lies in pre-empting obsolescence of own products (and practices) with new features, or new replacements, before the competition.

Established companies tend to become euphoric with their successes. The better the company, the more efficient its operations are, the more tightly it locks into its current operations. They cling to their products and pour resources into existing businesses, irrespective of promises. Creative destruction is one solution. Abandonment is another. Abandonment is the key to innovation. It frees resources. Continuous tracking of the relative technical performances of the old and new approaches seems the only way to get timely warnings. General motors abandoned or completely made over six of their makes of automobiles and the result was tremendous growth.

The year 1980 witnessed the advent of mini computers that could perform some of the same functions as main frames; but at lower cost.

Collapse of sales of large main frame computers brought about a severe crisis in IBM, which once held more than 80 percent of the market in its grip. IBM held to its belief that the main frame market was due for growth. It was slow to react to the direction computing was taking, moving from hardware to chips and software. While competition dramatically reshaped them, IBM dithered. The indecision almost killed the company.

The Japanese have excelled the Swiss, in redesigning for quality, the watch business. They substituted inexpensive capacitor to compensate for variations in cheaper crystals and replaced expensive quartz crystal and Switzerland's legendary craftsmanship. Swiss share of global watch market dropped from 43 per cent in 1974 to less than 15 per cent in 1983.

Friggie International, with $ 1.3 billion in revenues in 1992, went in for a misguided $ 200 million investment in world class manufacturing through state-of-the-art technology conversions at all manufacturing facilities. It made an after tax loss of $ 166.7 millions in 1994. To diet the company back to health, it had to downsize, concentrating only on four core businesses and abandoning its territories of defeat. 1995 result showed return to profitability.

POOR COMMUNICATIONS

The common means of communication is *words.* However, if your message is not received, it is worthless. When you tell somebody to do something, the odds are that they did not understand you, for a whole lot of reasons. They may not have been attentive. They may have been thinking of something else (like going to the rest room). The expression in your face may have distracted them. Or, the words you used may not have been precise or meaningful. Communicating effectively involves keeping the message short and simple, precise and unambiguous. About 15 per cent of the words used are repeated frequently. Extra care in their choice would make the communication more effective.

Mis-communication results in misunderstanding, jealousy and friction between human beings. Or, interpreting it, as the receiver desires or taking it as understood. These are sources of unnecessary costs. An average Manager "spends 9 percent of his time writing, 16 percent in reading, 30 percent talking, 35 percent listening and the rest 10 percent on other activities" (Mudge, A.E., 1989). Faulty communication is not only expensive and time consuming, but also more importantly, a major source of poor actions and wrong decisions: and so, *poor value.*

Words are not the only means of communication. It is paradoxical that the natural gift of communicating without words is scarcely used except perhaps by the Japanese, who have made this into a fine art. Just as, the closeness that exists between a parent and the child, and the child, understanding everything just from a parent's glance, the Japanese Managers excel in getting a point across, communicating what is to be read from the situation and the context, by subtle body postures and unstated feelings.

There are about 6,800 languages world wide. Of these 6,000 are spoken by just one tenth of the world. The odds are that 50 to 90 per cent could become extinct by the end of the century. Even that would leave several languages in vogue all over the world. Fortunately, half the world is conversing in 15 languages. Even that is too much when seen against potential for errors in communication.

English is the common language within international business. Though it has two million words, it is full of pitfalls. For 500 most commonly used words there are 4,070 different dictionary definitions. In addition:

- English is notoriously illogical. For example, "tongue" is pronounced as "tung," but "argue" is not "arg" "Enough" is "enuff," but "bough" is not "buff." "Cough" is "cuff," but "bough" is "bow." English has 1,120 different ways of spelling its 40 phonemes - sounds required to pronounce all its words.
- Further, many words mean differently, when used in different contexts. For example: "wise man" and "wise guy" are opposites. Weather is as "hot as hell" one day and as "cold as hell" the next. One "recites at a play" and "plays at a recital." It is possible to "ship by truck," but only "send cargo by ship."
- Some words are confusing. There is no "egg" in an "egg plant:" neither "pine" nor "apple" in "pineapple." "Guinea pig" is neither a "pig," nor is it from "Guinea." "Quick sand" works slowly. "Boxing rings" are square. "Quite a lot" and "Quite a few" are alike. So also, a "slim chance" and a "fat chance."

- There is a lot of variation in the way English is spoken by different people. This phenomenon is called *"mother tongue influence."* To suppress these pronunciations, *"accent neutralization"* has to be done.
- There are also nuances in dealing with speech and cultural habits. Americans look for a *"yes or no"* answer to their queries. Asians, on the other hand, are prone to be apologetic and evasive. They have to be taught to say *"no,"* when the need arises.

Many foreign language translations are required for doing business worldwide. Not merely for traditional advertising and sales promotions, but for technical brochures, reports, specifications, standards, maintenance and service manuals, parts catalogues, labels and packaging, safety instructions, training manuals, contracts, patents, process control computer software, etc. Literally, there is a globe full of potential for errors.

One in every seven human beings can speak English. However, there are many who do not understand it - especially when used on the warning labels on equipment. This has led to people drowning when scuba diving, injuring the eye with a nail driver and getting badly burnt with a propane gas tank exploding in their face, despite mandatory warning labels affixed to them. The need for more effective communication through labels cannot be over emphasised. It carries major implications for the way public is warned about the hazards. Perhaps, a better mode of communication of the warnings may be to use pictures, pictograms, icons, signs, and the like.

Everybody claims to know what *"function"* means – the action for which anything exists. It is difficult for them to visualize *"the essence of the action for which the thing exists, expressed in two words - one, an action verb and the other, a measurable noun."*

PREJUDICE

Everyone is prejudiced in some way or the other. Prejudices influence opinions and attitudes - against a material, a certain method, a process, a person or an idea.

Years back, the Advisory Committee to Ferdinand and Isabella of Spain, was prejudiced that no one would find new lands, after so many centuries of creation. Vasco da Gama discovered the East and Columbus, America.

The telephone was invented in 1876. However, Western Union rejected the rights to telephone in 1876 as inherently of no value. Reportedly, their internal memo said, "this telephone has too many short comings to be seriously considered as a means of communication. What use could the company make of an electrical toy?" It did not go into widespread use in USA until 1940s. People were prejudiced that it was unnatural to have a conversation on the telephone. It was de-humanising.

Marshal Ferdinand Foch, the French Military strategist, had found "no military value" for airplanes, in 1911.

For Years, Indian Railways used to specify high-grade acid steel for engine and wheel set axles. This expensive steel had to be made by time consuming, and low yield, triplex process, in Acid Bessemer, Basic Open Hearth and Acid Open Hearth combination. The Railways were, at the same time, using the less expensive, easily produced basic steel, for wheels. They were prejudiced against the process of making basic steel by the Bessemer Converter, blowing air through the molten pig iron for rapid oxidation of metallics. Therefore, the insistence on high-grade acid steel, refined in open hearth, for axles. It took quite some research, development, experimentation and negotiation (involving considerable time and money) before the Railways agreed to use basic steel for axles on which the wheels of basic steel were mounted.

When Jamsetji Tata proposed to build a steel plant in India, in early 1900s, Sir Frederick Upcott, the then Chairman of the Railway Board, offered to eat every pound of steel rail the Indians succeed in making.

MISCONCEPTIONS

All of us have misconceptions. Only, they may be few or many, depending on our alertness to assimilate developments, as they occur and to correct our earlier experience.

In 1895, Dr. Simon Newcomb, the celebrated astronomer and Lord Kelvin, the President of Royal Society, are said to have asserted that heavier-than-air flying machines are unpractical and insignificant, if not utterly impossible. The next year, the Wright Brothers succeeded at Kitty Hawk, USA.

In 1899, Charles Duell, head of US Patent Office, observed that everything that would be invented had been invented.

In 1920, Robert Millikan, co-founder of quantum mechanics, declared that there is no likelihood that man would ever tap the power of the atom.

To Thomas Watson, Chairman of IBM, is attributed the remark, "there is a world market for may be five computers." More recently, Ken Olsen, founder of Digital Equipment, held that there is no reason for any individuals to have a computer in their home.

In 1958, British Ambassador Dr. R Woolsey, pronounced space travel as utter bilge.

Churchill considered Indians incapable of taking care of the country, running it and ruling it. So, he refused to grant Independence.

Events proved that these were misconceptions.

Iron ships were thought to sink in water because of their weight. They would not float. They would damage more than wooden ships when grounded. Besides, they would be difficult to protect from rust. The navigational aid, the compass, would be deflected by the steel and make it useless for navigation. Another example: for years, steel was considered the only strong reinforcement, until polymers of equal strength were developed.

As regards quality, there are many: that quality improvement is limited to products; that it is just another program; that the responsibility for quality resides in the Quality Control/Inspection Department; that the process should be implemented by this department.

A company marketing baby food in Central Africa desired to boost sales. Because the literacy rate was practically zero, they thought of using pictures. They put a picture of a cute baby from the local tribe on the baby food jar. The customers responded; but not the way the company expected. The customers misconceived that the picture on the jar represented its contents, and concluded that the baby food contained processed baby.

LACK OF EXPERIENCE

"Experience is a wonderful thing; it enables you to recognise a mistake every time you repeat it" (Anonymous). Only, how many do so?

When Edison was developing incandescent light, he went through 9000 experiments to produce the bulb. His associates called them failures. However, Edison held that he had not even failed once. He had learnt 9000 times, what does not work.

All of us are prisoners, to one degree or another, of our experience. Often, when we talk of 25 years experience, it actually is one year's experience multiplied twenty-five times.

The combination, of experience, information, reason and intuition, is powerful. Real experience is a process of discovering and learning something new, which somehow leads to a growing cumulative capability. In this sense, even failures will add to one's storehouse of experience, if the venture was creative. When Du Pont was working on polymer chemistry, the aim was to manipulate the structure of large, organic molecules. One failure found the stuff in the kettle congealed into fibers. Thus was born nylon.

In the Seventies, consultants identified global scale and experience effects as essential advantages to be pursued. Several industries made investments in large-scale plants, hoping to enlarge their market shares. What actually transpired was over capacity and drastic price reduction.

DESIRE TO CONFORM

Every company has a tradition of operation, a culture and a product line, which they follow year in and year out. Like, Avis's car rental that tries harder (than Hertz); Caterpillar that view dealers as partners; Wells Fargo Bank's Five Dollars or Five Minutes; and IBM's best service. They conform to pursue these goals.

Normal industry work and day to day duties also involve conformance to practices, procedures and policies. Here, conforming stems from fear of the unknown. A known devil is better than the unknown; so, conform.

Nonconformity, both intellectually and personally, appears to be a central characteristic of the highly creative. A healthy disregard for conventional thinking seems to be good, as the following examples show.

For nearly a century, Ford conformed to their traditional, geography based, production system of designing cars in local markets and prospered, selling in 1993, five of the best vehicles in USA. However, despite this record, Alex Trotman, revamped operations in April 1995 to build world cars. He merged American and European operations into one global unit, with 5 vehicle centres- one in Europe and four in Dearborn - to design, develop and engineer vehicles with a single set of processes for product development and common manufacturing systems. His Ford 2000 had common components that can be sold worldwide, with minor styling changes to appeal to customers in local markets. He calculated that this dramatic and quick change would gain for Ford a market sweep in Asia, which today has 80 percent of the world's population, but only 8 percent vehicle sales.

South West Airlines, USA, has remained the most consistently safe, reliable and profitable airline in USA for the past 30 consecutive years. It does not conform to the expensive hub and spoke airline industry conventions. The airline has no reserved seats, flies only one type of aircraft: the Boeing 737s, and operates short haul, but frequent flights. It performs such feats as a 15 minute plane turn around-one third of the industry average - with crews 50 percent smaller than the competition. This low fare airline generates more revenue and more passengers per employee than any other airline. It has a humanised workplace, where work is fun and the line between fun and work are blurred and fuzzy. It expects to be "solidly profitable" in the future.

Gage Talker Corporation, tiny manufacturer of data collection software, but not the hardware it runs on, made the customer-driven decision to design and make the PC needed by the customers. This was balking the conventional wisdom that says only a big company can compete in the PC market. The product is now on backlog. The company is predicted to double within a year.

Institutional investors and compensation critics have held that effective leadership and excellence will be in direct proportion to the personal stakes that CEOs, Directors and top Executives hold in the company. By nonconforming to these norms, some companies have demonstrated their full commitment to increasing shareholder value, as their number one priority. Example: Tata Steel, the top steel plant in India for decades, where Tatas hold less than 3 percent stakes, the Government institutions, 46 percent and 8,000 shareholders, the rest.

POOR INTERACTION AMONG CONTRIBUTING DISCIPLINES

Traditionally, companies specialise in their industry and individuals, in their careers. To achieve right results to a given purpose (product or production) specific responsibilities are assigned to specialist professionals: like, production, materials, finance, engineering, markets, personnel, etc. They are set into work units or organisational blocks. This block concept is so deeply rooted that each specialist and his department then endeavour to take responsibility for that area alone. They work at legitimate cross-purposes, governed by self-interest and own sub-goals. For example, the Designer, equating his best performance to engineering excellence in terms of materials, precision in manufacture, performance, strength and reliability, would tend to make the product stronger, larger and heavier than necessary; and, consequently, costlier. He does not look at the design from the standpoint of the production work. The proposed design could be beyond the capacity and capability of existing equipment, process and skills. The Production Manager, in his zeal to maximise efficiency, would avoid idling of men and machinery, and wastage of material and minutes (time). He would favour fewer models, longer production runs, minimum and simpler set-ups, etc. to keep his cost low. It may not be the optimum combination or cost to produce, or the source of excellent opportunities for selling. The Materials Manager, seeing his job as getting the best material at the lowest price and best delivery from the registered suppliers, would not exploit to advantage equally good or better alternatives in specification or supplier. He would like to place larger orders to get price discounts and save on replenishment costs; and incur increased inventory cost. The Sales would give away discounts and promise ex-stock deliveries to fatten their order books. These affect adversely cost of production, work schedule and even quality (while rushing orders through the system), to redeem their promises. Traditionally, each specialist would pursue his sub-goal with ardour, but the sum total of all such pursuits may not, and need not, add up to the goals and expectations of the organisation: customers' value.

Their approaches may not be in synergy. Each department works on its own logic and wants to protect that logic. For example, Research may wish to develop the best-engineered products; but those products may not sell at that high quality level and prices. The Materials manager may look for "the lowest price" for "good enough supplies," to specification; but Production would have problems to manufacture with them; or the customers, to maintain. Transportation may like rail over air as the lower-cost shipping mode; but, the customers will be forced to wait longer for the items. Marketing may hold something the customers would not like. The Divisional Head, at the middle level, would look for "profitable solutions to a cost problem or a revenue generating opportunity." Top management would be less interested in solutions to problems than profits it can add or the improvement in productivity of corporate assets that it will permit. Accounts would press for reduction in support services or substitution of a lower cost ingredient "to save on costs." Which, the Sales, Production and Quality Control may see as "increasing customer discontent," and "leading to more operation/repair problems" respectively.

Their performance measures may not be aligned. Planning may emphasise growth; budgeting, earnings; and production, incentives. Their priorities may differ. One month production; another, quality; next, on labour saving or inventory control. Coupled with constraints like time horizons, uncertainty and limited resources, these tend to dilute focus.

Their satisfaction measures may differ. Employees would demand higher wages and perquisites; customers would look for lower prices; and better deliveries and shareholders would ask for higher prices and dividends.

Possessing advanced skills and spending their entire career with own specialty, they tend to develop sub-goals devoted to their specialties. They may lack system understanding. They may not appreciate enough the subtleties of other jobs; nor really see the inter-dependencies. They may not know either the people or their problems to help others. A major process would involve several departments and professional specialists. If they do not work towards a common goal, precious time would be lost. Acts of omissions and commissions would abound. Cooperation and coordination between specialties, if any exist, may only be in a distant and formal manner. Mistrust, withholding of information, defensive communication and unwillingness to change are common.

Sharing information is considered an affront to their expertise. Result: decisions, which could have been easily made, postponed. Because somebody thought that somebody else could not comply. Or, what could have been done; what could have been done easily; what was the obvious thing to do; was not done. On the other hand, Ford has one of the most successful, tried-and-proven schemes for knowledge sharing, called Best Practices Replication Process. In almost 5 years, more than 2,800 proven superior practices have been shared across Ford's manufacturing operations. It had netted a billion-dollar benefit for the auto maker. Royal Dutch/Shell and Nabisco have licensed the process.

As the market grows, companies try to satisfy every single customer (user) through the same product or service, adding progressively feature after feature, to become multi-purpose performer. In the process, they maximise what the product can do, rather than optimise for meeting a specific customer request. Simultaneously, the product or service costs more, becomes hard to use, maintain, repair and service - loss in value.

Larger the organisation, more complex it becomes; one part undoing what another part is doing. Contributing disciplines work without common direction, setting priorities to suit expediency, consuming resources (sometimes at the cost of others), becoming mutually incompatible over a range of work and non-work related issues.

COMFORTABLE HIGH COST ACTIVITIES

When some activities that go on well have remained in vogue for a long time, they become established as part of the organisation. Especially, if they intrinsically cost not too much. Nobody wants to, or has the time to, bother with them. Consequently, even if there are equivalent lower cost activities, they are not replaced. The unnecessary costs continue year after year.

CREEP

As the company ages, creep sets in. The company could become involved in several businesses, not originally planned to be in. The company could be making, in-house, many items, which were originally not available in the market. Currently, they may have become common items, and at lower costs. Age old, obsolete machinery, may be producing items "temporarily." Similar temporary changes made to solve some exigencies, or special needs, may have tightened specifications; and come to stay.

Changes in the normal operating procedures, made as temporary expedients, coupled with loose planning and/or lack of proper controls, cause creep to become permanent. Even, some side activities, or departments, edge into the main business, with consequent long-range effects. Looking closely into creep discloses operations, which should be outsourced.

Creep in product features and product cost occurs when Designers and approving authorities add something so that the product will be so much better or safer (cost only a little more). Or, when the fits are tightened a little bit, to err on the safe side. Or, like what a renowned pet food manufacturer did. They tested numerous packaging variables to make the product attractive to the purchaser. Everybody loved it - except the pets.

In the name of progress, often simple things are changed by creeping complications. For instance, take the TV remote. Once upon a time, the TV viewer had to operate only one on-off switch. Now, he or she has to coordinate three buttons on two remotes. Every upgrade now seems to be very complex and it downgrades the quality of life. Instead of forcing the customers to fit the equipment, it may be more valuable to make the equipment fit the customer.

This is best illustrated by the *post* 9/11 *mission creep.* Until 9/11, the system of screening before boarding the airplane was that developed by North West Airlines (in response to bombing of Pan Am Flight 103 over Lockerbie, Scotland). As a sequel to 9/11, the system was to be strengthened, to spot possible terrorists before they board the airplanes. A Computer Assisted Passenger Pre-screening System (CAPPS) was developed as replacement. However, what was intended to focus narrowly on terrorism in air-travel underwent several changes, intruding too much on peoples' privacy and getting bloated for a wide variety of broader police purposes. The Department of Homeland Security had to cancel the program, without implementing it. Now, they are seeking to introduce a modification, Secure Flight - CAPPS 2.

NON - VALUE - ADDING WORK

Just less than half the time spent on traditional design work is actually non-value-adding, as the work itself is caused by engineering changes. Parts are, on an average, designed twice. Once, as an initial release and second time, as a changed design. The changes usually snow ball. Yet, most are unnecessary. Recently, McKinsey analysed and found two thirds, in a case, unnecessary.

Poor procedures add up in cost. The number of approvals needed on documents would bear re-study and would be profitable. GE once did a post-mortem on a sampling of big mistakes. The review found that not one of them would have been prevented by an extra managerial signature.

Value added is defined as doing something to change the configuration during production, *i.e.,* the building and assembly process. Therefore, inspecting, testing, moving, storing, or manipulating the components that do not change the configuration, are non-value-adding. By the same token, administration and support activities are non-value-adding. The structure, the rules, the lines of authority and reporting, the procedures, etc., may inhibit value addition. The assumptions for values, if they continue to perform to the highest measure of competence, to take initiative and risks, to adapt to changes and to make decisions at the lowest levels in the organization, would bear review.

The aim would be to raise the value added contributions. Three courses of action are possible:

(i) Reducing non-value-adding work.

(ii) Re-designing the item to eliminate or reduce all costly value-adding work.

(iii) Maintaining balance between value-adding and non-value-adding activities.

Value Management and FAST are excellent tools to identify areas for improvement.

Proverbial non-value-adding work, leading to high costs, are in the Defense Services. Last year, Pentagon spent $ 409 on a sink that should have cost only $ 39. There were numerous other over priced items, like electric bells, springs, screws, screw thread inserts, etc.

Because cross company processes are not coordinated, a vast number of activities end up being duplicated. Same information is entered repeatedly into systems, same forms filled out and passed around many times, same checks, verifications and approvals, done over and over again, etc. This leads to inconsistencies, errors, misunderstandings, and non value-adding effort.

WASTE

During the last two centuries, vigorous industrialisation vastly enriched our world. However, in doing so, it also produced a rising tide of scrap, discards and waste. The world is beginning to cope with the environmental problems that are legacies of the past. Traditionally, industries are now embracing Govermental goals. Some companies have started to consider the environmental impact of their products and services over their entire life and that of their manufacturing processes. They are also examining the use of their dross as raw material and of redesigning the products to make them easier to use, recycle or incinerate. They wish to substitute cleaner technology.

As everything created must go somewhere, industry's traditional response was to recycle to the extent possible and dispose of the rest by incineration or releases into the atmosphere. They relied principally on waste disposal technologies, end-of-pipe controls, recycling and reuse. Some tried redesigning products to make them easier to reuse, recycle or incinerate. Good enough so far, but of poor value, today. Waste is any work that does not add value to the customer. Every company must take a hard look at its processes and identify better ways to perform the necessary functions. All companies have fat and waste in their system and processes.

Hopefully, with the steps being now taken by the companies, every penny of waste will be wrung from the procurement system. However, other areas, with equal or more potential for saving, do exist for action. In fact, most companies could do well to downsize to right size. There are many avenues, important among which are improving the way the functions are performed; eliminating bureaucratic and redundant procedures; reducing the losses in the system, process, procedure and product; etc.

"Environmental protection" has supplanted "cleanliness" and value has shifted to "industrial ecology." Common practice is to find use for the bye products. Air pollution equipment produce powdery residue of calcium sulphate and fly ash. The former can find use vice gypsum in wall boards. Fly ash is used in concrete. Similarly boiler slag is used for abrasives. Beyond it, industry is now beginning to find that it makes sense to pass energy, waste water and some products back and forth between a number of plants (Kalundborg, Denmark); design products that are eco-friendly; and so on. Value has this shifted to elimination of releases that are hazardous and pollutants.

The notion that environment is just an expensive cost is out of date. Value based action proves that risking environmental benefits can be also profitable. Starbucks *(coffee par excellence)* are growing coffee plants under a forest canopy (and not in open ground), saving trees that would normally be cut and preventing rain forest carnage. The coffee beans so grown add to quality of the beverage. Nova Chemicals set aside 11.5 acres out of its 60 acre plot, for a habitat for migratory birds. The one time cost is about $ 8,000 to plant 24 species of trees and fruit bearing shrubs. The unanticipated savings, in not mowing those 11.5 acres, is $ 16,000.

Returns have become an inevitable nuisance, especially with the growth in e-commerce. On an average 6 percent of retail sales are returned by American customers, per year. The lowest is 2 percent for automobile parts; and the highest, 40 percent for women's apparel. In the past, it was enough for the return centres to recycle them, to salvage, repair and re-use to the maximum extent possible. Additional value is found by some by selling in outlet centres or abroad or by re-boxing them for the next season or sale theme. However, now value here has shifted to cost prevention - by providing testing and analysis to determine why the product has a high rate of return.

Estimates vary on what money is wasted buying unnecessary insurance. Such wastage can occur in two ways - paying too much; and buying policies that are not needed. Because of unrealistic fears and inadvertent duplication of what is already covered unwanted policies are purchased.

SHAPE A WINNER

In what follows, a preliminary estimate of what steps can, and should, be taken to enhance value and thus shape a winner, are given in brief.

Why Poor Value	*Prescription to Improve Value*
I. Lack of Information	• With right information, one can do almost anything. • Vital information comes from free, frank interaction among internal functions, employees, customers, external associates, etc. • Focus and re-focus information to improve performance. • Use Best Practices Replication. • Bring information age capabilities to everyone. • Days of hope, belief and surmises are long past. The need today is for precise information-interrelated and on numerical basis.
2. Lack of Knowledge	• Knowledge comes from information. • Maintain updated data on relative profitability of items (especially production, cost standards, etc.) • Ideas are key to success. Start an idea bank. • Use data bases in Internet.
3. Lack of Time	• Practice time management. • Demand fast responses. • Set example.

Contd....

Why Poor Value	*Prescription to Improve Value*
	• The message is in the time spent on each item.
	• Make most of the time. Method will teach how to win time.
	• As you will not find time for anything, if you want time, you must make it.
4. Lack of Attention	• Errors to become unacceptable.
	• Be prepared for every exigency.
	• Insist on value in everything done and made.
5. Lack of Listening	• Effective listening is engaged listening. Practice it.
	• Use all listening techniques.
6. Lack of Problem Ownership	• No postmortems to fix blame.
	• Investigate what went wrong and fix it.
	• Encourage people taking up more and more tasks, as needed.
7. Poor Quality	• Quality to standards is basic, not a matter of choice. Build requisite quality into design. Engineer it into the process, product and service.
	• Quality is conformance to requirement; not mere goodness.
	• There has to be something that distinguishes the product or service from what it already was.
	• Use as measure customer perceived quality.
	• Check quality per cost.
	• Maintain quality affordability.
8. Honest Wrong Beliefs	• Nothing is predictable.
	• Predicting the future is an exercise in delusion.

Contd....

Why Poor Value	*Prescription to Improve Value*
	• Future belongs to a well organised and value-focused company.
	• No firm can take anything for granted.
	• Check, understand and then only act.
9. Habitual Thinking	• Habit solutions are unacceptable.
	• Let go of the old situation.
	• Go through the neutral zone between old reality and new reality that may still be unclear. Adjust and be reborn.
10. Risk of Personal Loss	• Practice saving face.
11. Reluctance to Seek Advice	• Admit when you do not know the answer.
	• Seek advice of experts.
12. Habits and Attitudes	• Eschew habit solutions.
	• Cultivate devotion to basics .
	• Nurture positive attitude towards people and for adding value.
	• Foster participation, cooperation and relationships.
	• Control by simple support systerns, aimed at measuring right parameters.
	• There is tremendous power in a ritual. Tap into the power of rituals for cultivating good habits.
13. Unrealistic Requirements	• Refrain from specifying unnecessary excesses in factors of safety, allowances, tolerances, fits and finishes, treatments, etc.
	• Attach money value to each requirement; compare, before specifying.
	• Challenge to determine actual requirement.

Contd....

Why Poor Value	*Prescription to Improve Value*
14. Temporary or Changed Circumstances	• Beware of temporary solutions. They become permanent. • Stable mass production relies on cutting labour costs. Instead, increase labour value. • Change from mass marketing to pin point marketing. • Look for inconsistencies and eliminate them.
15. Changing Technology	• Expanding knowledge and advancing technology impact on everything. It blurs and enhances product (and service) distinction. • Keeping a technology requires elaborating upon it continuously, developing variations and small improvements, to better meet specific needs. • Search and exploit new opportunities. • Continuously introduce innovations in small steps.
16. Poor Communications	• Whenever you communicate, make sure the receiver understands it fully and well. • Keep messages short, simple, precise and unambiguous. • Devote extra care in choice of words. • Use other modes (besides words).
17. Prejudice	• Do not expect perfection. Accept the best. • Focus on nurturing ideas.
18. Misconceptions	• Economies of scale and shifting operations to lower labour cost countries, are worth less everyday. Other methods should be preferred.

Contd....

Why Poor Value	Prescription to Improve Value
	• Big is not necessarily the best. • Consider labour as an ally, not as cost, or a mechanical tool, to be greatly specialised or replaced by labour saving devices. • Required, not mere efficiency, but efficiency cum effectiveness. • Better value is in optimisation, not maximisation. • Many ideas have become out of date. Re-examine them to take value-oriented action that could be profitable. • Your profitability, customer value, share holder wealth, employee satisfaction, move in lock step.
19. Lack of Experience	• The combination of experience, information, reason and intuition, is powerful. • Learn from failures as much as from successes. • Learn from the experience of others. • Every answer to every problem can be found in print, somewhere. Search for it. • Use people as prime source of value addition. Train, empower, involve. Retool.
20. Desire to Conform	• Foster non-conformity to encourage creativity. • Contradicting prevailing conventional wisdom has also succeeded. • Make value the goal.
21. Poor Interactions between Department and between Specialists	• Strip down functional barriers. • Use team approach - preferably self-directed teams.

Contd....

Why Poor Value	*Prescription to Improve Value*
	• Make staff functions to support the line. • Train, empower, involve. • Use people as prime source of value addition. • Seek synergy.
22. High-Cost Activities	• Look for and eliminate duplication of efforts. • Improve applications. • Review all activities periodically for their contribution to value.
23. Creep	• Review all activities periodically for their contribution to value. • Review out-sourcing *vs* in-house production.
24. Non Value-Adding Work	• Check overheads. • Check number of approvals per document. • Check cross company processes for duplicated efforts.
25. Waste	• Curb all wastes. • Search for, identify and eliminate hidden wastes. • Review current waste disposal work. • Intensify recycling, reuse and bye product utilisation. • Explore ways of preventing scrap, releases and pollutants. • Explore also how to convert them into valuable, usable materials, leaving no residue. • Check returns and recalls to determine why, and why at that rate. Rectify the causes. • Watch out for time waste and unnecessary use of resources.

CREATE, BUILD AND ADD VALUE

- Opportunities for Correction
- The Company's Value Chain
- Techniques to Assist
- Options for Action
- External Value Chain
- Customers' Value Chain
- Suppliers' Value Chain
- Channel Value Chain
- Stake Holder Value

5 CREATE, BUILD AND ADD VALUE

Organised efforts to obtain high value were, so far, an exception, rather than the rule.

In the past, the industries' principal concerns were production and the critical uncertainties crucial to production. Their immediate concern was not for stretching the boundaries of current opportunities, but, to keep up with the demands. However, to be more efficient at what they do, they developed progressively superior tools and skills of operational improvement. They improved planning, execution, control and discipline - needed to serve the ready market with current products, as such.

Almost all current products and services are concepts of manufacturers, not of customers. The manufacturers conceived the idea, specified what goes into it, and how to make it, and offered it to the customers. As such, the product or service seldom matched fully the customers' requirements and needs. That is, even when market surveys and prototype testing preceded the decisions and customer feed backs resulted in corrections. Design engineering and manufacturing preferences overrode customers' advantages. With a sellers market almost, none thought in terms of redesigning existing products with appropriate improvements necessary to satisfy customer needs more effectively. Neither, for producing new products, better suiting customer needs.

This would be the first step for value enhancement: to study what the customers do not like among current products and understand well their actual needs and requirements, articulated or otherwise. Knowledge of the benefits of value to the customers would pave the way to innovate and pre-empt others in delivering those benefits.

For any company, its product (or service); the work structure and system that makes it; the current market that consumes it; the margins between prices and costs; as well as the assets and skills that generate the margins; together constitute the profit generator. Comparative improvements in any of these areas made by a competitor become threats. That is when the company usually searches for ways and means to raise, or add, new levels of performance and service. Attention then focuses on two major areas - firstly, on raising the past bench marks of operations (internally generated measures, norms and assumptions); and secondly, on catching up with others (on technology, efficiency, productivity, yield, quality, costs, and so on). Here again, focus is not for dealing with the fundamental issues that led to the crisis. Not for creating highly distinguished products or services that can sell for much more than what they cost to produce. Not for building the responsiveness necessary to satisfy the minute differences in demand. Nor, for making continuous improvements or innovations, in every thing, by every employee. So, the next step in sequence would be value studies, to identify possible remedies here.

It is human nature to choose the easier way out of knotty situations. The legacy of factory system and the financial measures of control, designed for mass, scale, and specialisation, make cutting down direct labour the easier route to better productivity and economies. A means for trimming off excesses that it is, it helps only survival; not growth, neither morale, nor creativity. Resources and lean organisation cannot substitute creativity. Therefore, training to manage for value, the next step, is both necessary and urgent, for implementing remedial action.

Value, higher order values, new levels of values and delivered to customers, reign crucial to success, more than ever before. Value Engineering, as it was originally structured, had concentrated on achieving the product's purpose, at the required standard of quality and reliability, and at an acceptable cost. The focus was on what the product must do - its functionality, quality reliability, and cost. They were some vital areas. However, the technique was not applied to either ends of the value adding continuum or the channels in the system. Nor did it take a holistic approach to improve values.

There are as many value-enhancing opportunities as there are meanings and perceptions of value; and value chains; and relationships. Managing for values is an attempt to systematise current approaches and extend the scope to cover the total horizon.

OPPORTUNITIES FOR CORRECTION

Opportunities are numerous, for correction, to maximise value. Every cause of poor value, discussed in Chapter 4, is a challenge for action and an opportunity for correction to create, build and add value. For each cause, a general prescription for correction to improve value, is given in the foregoing section: Shape a Winner. Analytical techniques described in it would assist in identifying the value enhancing opportunities. The enormous scope for action would be evident from the range of techniques suggested in this section.

A company can be seen as a collection of resources (technological, technical, financial, human and so on). With these resources, it performs several discrete conceptual, physical and technological activities: like, designing, manufacturing, assembling, processing, controlling, selling and distributing. Its human resources (men and management) use technology (equipment, process and procedures) to convert purchased inputs (raw materials, semis and components) into items of value (product or service) to satisfy customer needs (use, performance and costs). This is schematically shown in Fig. 5.1.

The arrows represent the interactions - threats and internal pressures that impact these activities.

How each activity is performed and its economics determine the cost of the product produced, the contribution to customer needs, and the service rendered by the company.

All activities, processes, procedures, etc., must be put through a thorough examination of their usefulness in terms of value they produce for the company – value that must be judged in terms of benefits to the customer or user. Examples of such multifunctional activities are product design, process design, logistics, manufacturing, distribution, customer service, etc. Analysing the customers' value chains, the company can often identify where in its own value chain it can specialise, maintain superiority and continually innovate. Superior skills, systems and competence in all these areas, allow it to serve the customers better.

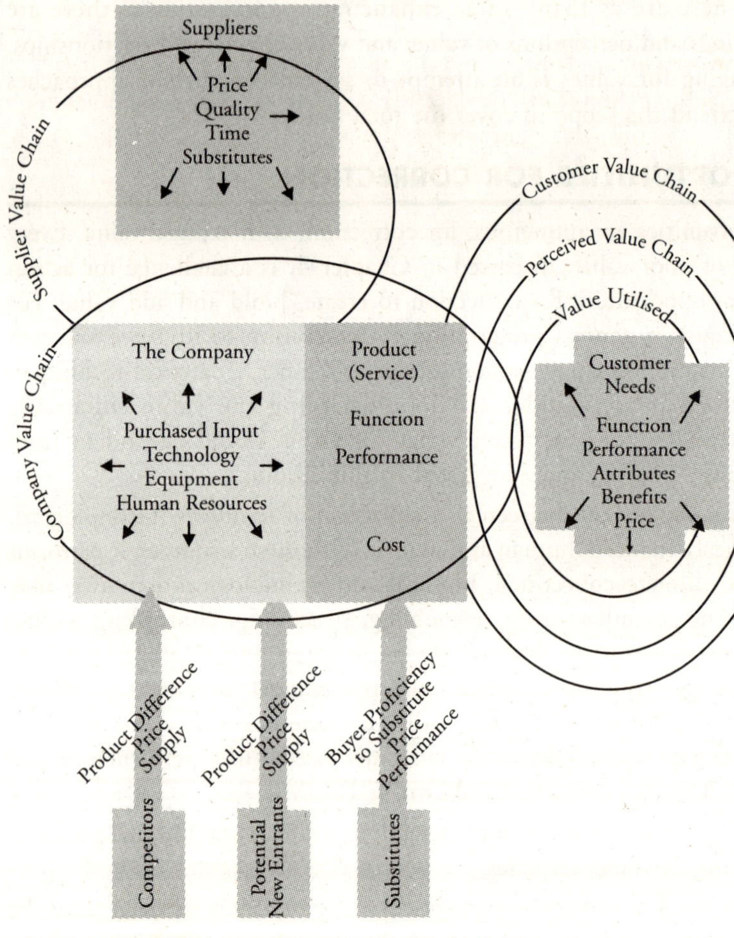

***Fig. 5.1 Threats and Internal Pressures influencing Survival, Growth and Profitability – Company's Value Chain**
*(*See coloured presentation at the end of the chapter)*

Alternatively, in select activities in the value chain, most critical to the company's success.

Determining where to focus one's resources internally and what to out - source would also be important. Where it has considerable knowledge of technology, process and equipment, as well as skills to produce, it can endeavour to excel. Where it cannot excel, collaborating with best-in-world external sources would be the way to maintain leadership.

Besides activities, processes, etc., all employees of all levels must also be assessed continuously for how their work adds value.

The company is also a collection of products and services, for making which it uses these activities. Any product or service can be transformed into a high value added item through accumulation of several small need-based advantages. For instance, Millikan turned the humble shop towel into a high value-added, greatly differentiated product. Whereas, companies seldom take full advantage of the state of the art, new materials, or new processes. Paucity of resources and time usually stand in the way of changes. Many opportunities arising out of changes in customer needs and markets go unexploited.

A product is the physical embodiment of a set of actions and services desired by the customers or users. The product has some configuration - form, line, shape, size, proportion; some esteem - colour, texture, finish; some efficiency; and a fair safety of operation. It performs, or is used to perform, some work. It has a life (durability). It would be possible to maintain it, repair it and service it. The relative importance of these factors would vary. A product is also a collection of tangible and intangible attributes and features. It is these configuration, attributes and features that the customer buys, for accomplishing a purpose or deriving a satisfaction with the product. A service is the product of someone's labour. It has some use; some life (duration of efficacy); availability and efficiency. Again, these are the attributes the customer buys, for accomplishing a purpose or deriving a satisfaction with the service.

What the attributes and features are, and in what quantity, quality, mix, combination, or configuration these are present, will determine the cost of the product produced or service rendered, and the differentiation with competitive offerings. Value screening and measurement techniques determine and quantify the value of attributes and features in any system. Numerical procedures translate subjective opinions and perceptions into objective properties, events, states and traits and provide estimates of their relative values. Modelling simulates changes over time of value of various items. Together, these aid to focus attention and decision-making, for action for improvement of the vital few.

Every four or five years, companies try to introduce a product variation. The conventional focus goes to maximising current functions, particularly efficiencies, yields, bringing down cost of variety and flexibility, customising, responding fast, etc. These represent only the tip of the iceberg of gains in differentiation. Every product, every service can be differentiated. Product features, attributes, properties, characteristics, performance, life, technology employed, quality of inputs, quality of treatments, skill and experience used, information base for controls - there are several avenues to change. Any change in any of the attributes and features influences performance, costs of production and the basis of differentiation - which in totality is value.

The company's total value offering is shown in red in Fig. 5.1. The goal of the company is to create and supply total value (product or service) for the customers that exceed the cost of production and supply.

As Fallon (Carlos Fallon, 1971) elucidates, "what a product is, what it does and what it costs are matters of fact. What it should be, what it should do and what it should cost are matters of value. High speed and low speed, large size and small size, high cost and low cost are matters of fact. The right speed, the right size and the right cost are matters of value. When the right is understood as right for a given purpose," the point of golden balance is struck. "Greater and less are matters of fact, achieved mainly through simple effort in a given direction. Better and worse are matters of value, requiring judgement to determine the direction in which effort should be applied to achieve best value."

THE COMPANY'S VALUE CHAIN

The company's value chain is all the work that must be done to design, produce and deliver a product or service to the customer and support it. The physical chain, starting with the raw materials, continuing through inbound logistics, production processes and ancillaries, control systems, outbound logistics, marketing, sales, distribution, and ending with after-sales services, represent the links. Fig 5.2 shows a typical value chain in a manufacturing company.

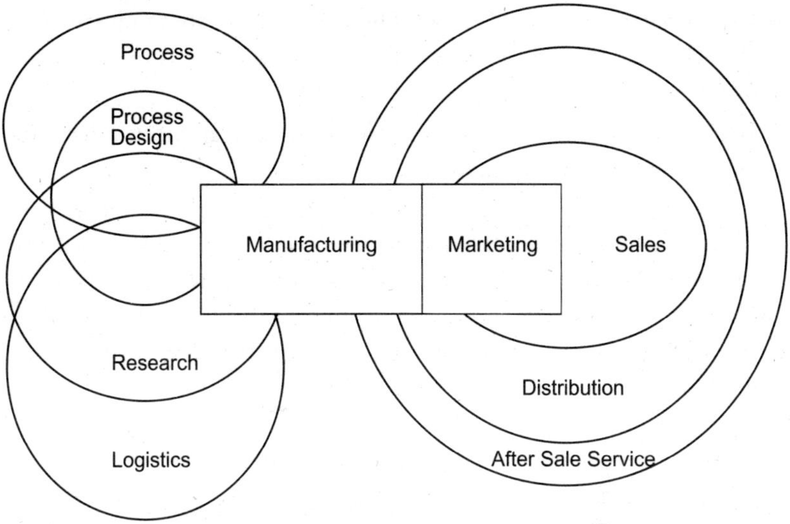

***Fig 5.2 Value Chain for a typical manufacturer**
*(*See coloured presentation at the end of the chapter)*

There is no industry today that is not technology-dependant. Technology is pervasive in the company's value chain. Every activity uses some technology, relevant machinery and needed human skills to convert inputs into products and services. By upgrading its technology or changing for a better technology, the company can secure comparative advantages in product (or service) performances, attributes, uses, costs and differentiation. Thus, it can improve its value chain. For instance, Nucor used a technological innovation to gain spectacular order of magnitude improvements within its value chain. Nucor replaced the traditional, capital intensive, time consuming and low efficiency, hot metal-ingot steel-rolling route of steel making with quicker, scrap-molten steel-continuous casting route. However, there are limitations. Discovery of new technology is unpredictable, being the result of genius and luck, and once in a life time occurrence. A new venture would profit from its use. One cannot ignore the reality of existing plants and process; and the economics of nurturing, extending, modifying or adapting them over their full life cycle. Any change in technology would lead to fewer people working on line in any operation centre. Those who remain at work will become more important to the company's success than ever before. Therefore, the organisation structure would also need changes to make every function fully committed and involved in the value-adding continuum.

Continuous introduction of technological innovations in small steps would be the feasible alternative.

A company provides specific skills and technologies to every element in its internal value chain. Some outsider, by specialising in an element, can become more proficient and pose a threat. The company must constantly assess its competence in all links, look beyond where it is currently best, to areas where it can be best or· where it must be best. That would provide the value leverage. To attain preeminence in any activity and sustain it, it must continually focus its resources to raise its value to the company and to provide unique value to the customers. The real challenge is to build dominant skill set in areas that the customer would value now and in the future.

Within the company, each activity, whether direct, indirect or support, affects, and is affected by, others, as regards performance and cost. For example, product design influences functionality, quality, reliability and cost. Materials management practices affect quality and delivery of purchased inputs, and hence, influence product quality, product cost and inspection costs. Tighter inspection of incoming items reduces quality assurance costs in the production process. On finished goods, it goes to improve reliability and reduce field service costs. Better maintenance lowers down time and saves in production costs. Frequent deliveries reduce inventory and accounts receivable. Product reliability may require more material use or more expensive materials, reflecting in costs. All these internal pressures (shown by arrows in Fig. 5.1) affect the company's value chain.

Normal industry effort is to maximise results in traditional functions. This may or may not add any value. For, once optimisation is reached, (say at between 75 percent and 80 percent of theoretical maximum), the costs of additional effort rise exponentially, while additional results decline, also exponentially. Departmental barriers, absence of interaction among the specialists and decades old attitudes, compound the problems (see also Chapter 4). Results are derived from multifunctional activities.

The quality of management decision-making contributes to the value created. Decision-making involves objective, alternatives and information. Different objectives, time horizons, uncertainty, limited resources and multiple priorities dilute the focus. Daily decision-making allocates resources (physical and human) and time. How well these are made and how consistent these are, affects value creation. When Managers face roadblocks, they lose focus on the goal. They focus on solving the roadblocks. Effective execution would come from focus and concentration of efforts on value drivers: product offering, mix, process work flow, logistics, cost, overheads, service and maintenance trade off, replacement and upgrade trade off, staff activities, collection procedure, sourcing, channels, etc. To have everyone and every activity focused in the right direction, nothing can excel value and value drivers. Obviously, removing deficiencies and improving the quality of decision and execution, would reflect as additions of new or higher values in activities or product.

Systems have become more important than ever, for value enhancement. Conventional systems channel information narrowly. They are biased towards control, especially efficiencies, yields and costs. They are not the best means for action to enhance effectiveness or value. Existing measurements tell only part of the story. They have to be correlated to value. Systems and measurements should encourage participation and understanding by everyone; and support initiative and execution by frontline staff. Where inadequate, steps need to be taken to correct. In value measurement techniques, one would find the solutions.

Products can be copied, easily reverse-engineered or replaced by substitutes. However, small incremental improvements that can transform a product or service over time will make all the difference in quality, life, performance, sales appeal, price, and acceptability by the customers. "There are as many strengths to build on as there are factors that matter to the customers in the products and services a company makes and delivers," (Clifford, D.K., 1985). Conventional measurement systems do not reflect important drivers of success: like product quality, customer satisfaction, responsiveness, flexibility, long-term costs of product development, etc. Identifying the drivers of performance, functionality and costs, and selectively controlling them, would ensure best results in the company's value-adding continuum.

Problems occur when concentrating too narrowly on products or too inflexibly on skills that no longer match customer needs. Flexible skill sets and constant reassessing of trends are necessary. Only then can a dominant skill be built in areas that the customer will continue to value in the future.

A firm's strategy for a given product or service is determined by the selling price, quality and functionality. The test of a toy is its "play value." That is not whether the child plays with the toy for a long time and uses it repeatedly. It is whether the child reverts to an old favourite, in preference to the new toy; and its frequency.

Companies competing on functionality and quality adopt differentiation strategies. The company's differentiation stems also from how its value chain relates to the value chains of the customer downstream, the supplier upstream, and the channels of distribution in between. These can be used to control the way technology diffuses through the different chains; and the rapidity of making innovations. The process begins with an understanding of the important interactions. Improving individual activities confer advantages both for themselves and for the linkage among activities. It enables coordination, modification and optimisation of performance of all activities by others so inter linked. Identifying and defining the value drivers and using them as sustainable sources for reconfiguring, or reinforcing the drivers of performance and counteracting drivers of cost, would favour not only the company, but all.

By analysing the customers' value chains, a company can often identify the activities in the value chain:

(i) most critical to the company's future success;

(ii) most critical to the customers' success;

(iii) where it has specialised or where it can specialise;

(iv) where it can improve function or lower costs;

(v) where it can capture all opportunities taking place with the customers and sell cost and performance improvements to them.

(vi) where it can serve customers better or more effectively than anyone else; and

(vii) which can contribute to competitive advantage.

Products that are undifferentiated in value become commodities. It pays handsome dividends to differentiate by developing unique products and services that closely satisfy specific customers' needs, lowering customers' costs, or improving customers' performance - the value of the market place. Nurture activities that earn above average returns, which reflect their successes at achieving improved values. Examples: Gas stations offer not only petrol, but also a variety of choices: pricing, self-service or full service, repairs, parts, car wash, convenience stores, fast food restaurants, diesel fuel, air, Automatic Teller Machines, and so on. Each has a cost factor and a customer value. Heinecken pays particular attention to the quality and purity of the ingredients of its beer and uses a constant strain of yeast.

Differentiation sets an item apart from its competitor. But, concentration on points of differentiation alone may not suffice to add value. What is needed is a reassessment of the points of parity from time to time. Because, attributes that were once differentiators can become minimum requirements. Walking away from established positions and investing too heavily on points of difference can foster competition to copy and/or leap frog. Signalling to customers about the goals they can expect to achieve from your product or service (features and attributes) is important.

Whatever the customers buy has to fit their realities or it is of no use to them. "A firm's product eventually becomes part of its buyer's value chain," (Porter, M.E., 1985). Miles clarifies, it is fundamental that "an acceptable product must serve the customers' needs and wishes to the degree that he or she expects," (Miles, L.D., 1971). Miles terms this *performance capability*. Performance is the specific combination of functional abilities and properties that make it suitable and saleable for a specific purpose. Appropriate performance requires that the products (or services) have a predetermined level of quality, reliability, durability, interchangeability, appearance and maintainability; and that it satisfies all of these requirements of that level at a reasonable cost. For a desired function there are infinite permutations and combinations of material, process, design, configuration, method, means, etc; each with its performance and cost characteristics (refer Fig. 3.2). As the world progresses, many more are added. Therefore, at any point of time, there will be more than one way to optimise the parameters of performance, service, differentiation, cost and customisation for current and future customers. That is what Honda is trying to do when, "along with their world-renown cars, they manufacture some of the world's most reliable motor cycles, marine engines, generators, snow blowers, lawn mowers, all-terrain vehicles and tillers." Products are designed to balance customer requirements, needs for better fuel efficiency and cleaner air.

TECHNIQUES TO ASSIST

There are several analytical techniques to identify and develop value-enhancing opportunities. As pointed out earlier, Value screening and measurement techniques determine and quantify the value of attributes and features in any system. Numerical procedures translate subjective opinions and perceptions into objective properties, events, states and traits, providing estimates of their relative values. Modelling simulates changes over time of value of various items.

Some useful techniques are:

- Function Analysis:
  - What does it do?
  - What must it do?
  - Where is it done?
  - Where must it be done?
  - Is it necessary?
- Requirements Analysis:
  - Why is it done?
  - What for is it done?
  - Is the requirement valid?
- Re-engineering Analysis:
  - How is it done?
  - How else can it be done?
  - What improvements can be made?
- Best Practice Analysis:
  - Best-in-world practice.
  - Best-in-industry practice.
  - Best-in-company practice.

- Cost Analysis:
  - What does it cost?
  - What must it cost?
  - What is the cost of alternatives?
  - What is the meaningful cost?
- Organisation Analysis:
  - Who does it?
  - Who else can do it?
- Productivity Analysis:
  - What are the steps?
  - What are their costs?
  - What are the times?
  - How can they be reduced?
- Customer Analysis:
  - What is wanted now?
  - What will be wanted in future?
  - Can the customer discern minor differences in
    - Quality?
    - Functionality?
    - Price?
- Competitive Analysis:
  - Who are the competitors?
  - What will be their future offerings?
  - What is their style -leading, or me-too producer?
- Life Cycle Analysis:
  - What is the life cycle?
  - What is the life cycle cost?
  - What is the rate of recovery of up front cost?
- Location Analysis:
  - Where is it done?
  - Why there?
  - Where else can it be done?
  - What will it cost to change?

OPTIONS FOR ACTION

The options for action to maximise value, using the Equation 3.2 are:

$$\text{Value} = \frac{F\,max}{C\,min} \quad \text{or} \quad \frac{F\uparrow}{C} \quad \text{or} \quad \frac{F}{C\downarrow} \quad \text{or} \quad \frac{F\uparrow}{C\downarrow} \qquad (5.1)$$

1. **Accomplishing equivalent or better performance at same or lower cost - upgrading product performance.**

Required level of performance at least cost, or the highest level of performance for a given cost, or an optimum compromise between the two.

Substitute, eliminate, combine, simplify; alter design, materials, process; and so on. Treat every product, process and activity, as something to be constantly made a little better, everyday, using every employee skill. Make that contribute to the customers' well being.

Determine what is satisfactory performance; where it ends; and where excess performance begins. Relate performance to functions - Basic and Secondary. In the market place, those functions will survive which have use value.

Use Function Analysis, FAST Diagram, Numerical Evaluation, Process Flow Charts, Multi-Activity Chart, Work Simplification, etc.

Review the function(s) - Improve the Basic Function. Creatively develop alternatives to satisfy the Basic Function at the lowest possible total cost. Limit the number and cost of necessary Secondary Functions. The aim is to build in the item only the best Basic Function or the best Basic Function plus the inescapable minimum Secondary Function.

Plastics and aluminum are replacing much of steel in car building now, than ten years ago. The use of an aluminum block and molded-nylon intake manifold helped trim 55 Ibs. off the traditional iron cylinder block engine. Per vehicle, aluminum content has risen to 250 Ibs. reducing overall weight by 35 percent and costs by 14 percent. Cost wise steel: plastic: aluminum is as 1:2:4.5. Weight wise, it is 1:4:2.

Toyota made Lexus equivalent to a Mercedes Benz class luxury automobile, at affordable price for the average customer.

Arrows in equation indicate enhancement or improvement.

2. **Providing the shape, appearance, attractiveness and the features the customer wants - improving product esteem.**

Customers buy the functional product for their use value. Beyond functionality, they would also buy utilitarian items even if they do not need them, provided that thereby their quality of life is improved. Or, if it gives them some emotional satisfaction. Or, at least, it offers some raise in status. They would buy things even for indulgences, like taking care of self. Improving product esteem would mean making life's little luxuries more affordable for the not-so-rich classes.

Esteem value is difficult to quantify. However, improving it would pay dividends, especially when items have been in use for a long period of time and breakthroughs are imminent, as in the case of automobiles.

Miniaturise, combine, and streamline products.

Stampings have replaced fabrication and welding; plastics, many applications in steel; cellophane, polyester, plastic air bubble wraps, etc., many packaging requirements; paints, several finishing operations; and welds, fasteners. Stamped steel parts have been substituted for cast aluminum and magnesium, cutting production costs.

3. **Raising (or holding) necessary quality, at same (or reduced) cost, or both.**

$$\text{Value} = \frac{Q}{C} \quad \text{or} \quad \frac{Q\uparrow}{C} \quad \text{or} \quad \frac{Q}{C\downarrow} \quad \text{or} \quad \frac{Q\uparrow}{C\downarrow} \qquad (5.2)$$

Twenty years ago, quality was a major differentiator. With deregulation, globalisation of trade and adoption of world standards, all products are well on the way to equality of quality. Quality will soon cease to be a source of differentiation. However, it will remain forever a measure of customers' perception of excellence.

All quality being relative, each day, each product or service must get relatively better. "Almost all quality improvements come from simplification - of design, manufacturing, layout, process and procedures," (Peters, TJ., 1988). Therefore, quality improvement would also remain a never-ending journey.

Many products are now made in modules and can be added on to standard units. In automobiles, many features, earlier offered as optional extras over base price, are standard offerings.

Arrows in equation indicate enhancement or improvement.

Use Quality Function Deployment, TQM, Quality Affordability Matrix.

4. **Identifying and removing unnecessary costs and non-essential elements - cost prevention or cost avoidance, in addition to cost reduction.**

Check for functions, functional elements. Use Performance Cost Matrix, Cost Analysis, Break Even Charts, etc.

Maytag, redesigning its dishwasher line in 1992, changed the decade old design of the tub material from porcelain enamel steel to molded polypropylene. Besides reducing sheet metal work and metal scrap, it also gave collateral benefits: it eliminated porcelain finishing and solved the more vexatious and expensive problem of disposing the non-recyclable finishing residue and sludge.

5. **Exploiting all current changes (technical developments, expanding knowledge and "new" items) to advantage - Creativity and Innovation.**

Nicholas Hayak, with his Swatches, recaptured for the Swiss, the global market for inexpensive watches that they had lost to the Japanese. He reduced the usual number of parts by half, building them directly into the plastic casing on automated assembly lines. He kept direct labour under 10 percent, in contrast to the conventional 30 percent for most watch making operations.

In the offing is Bellcore's lightweight flexible rechargeable plastic battery that could revolutionise design of portable consumer electronic products such as toys, pagers, games, personal digital accessories, etc. It could even drive development of new devices capitalising on its from. It could make the electric car a viable product.

Find value, where there appears to be none; add value, where it is not substantial.

6. **Preventing unnecessary use of resources.**

Resources, through their concentrated application, accumulation, combination, conservation, re-use and rapid recovery, can be made to yield better returns.

CNN provides 24-hour world news on less than one fifth of what it costs CBS to produce one hour of news with their super star anchors and super star salaries.

The J-I-T/TQC message is that we should try to get by with less resources for everything: like, less set up time; less inventory; less inspection; less work in progress; less control; less paper work and comparing; less elaborate equipment; less specialization and less wastage. Remember, computers make it easy to do a lot of things. But, be cautious, as most of the things they make it easier to do, need not, perhaps, be done at all.

Most companies assume that they are already using the least expensive materials and most cost effective processes. Their current practices may include many that are based on age old ideas and beliefs that have not been updated for contemporary technological advances and changes. Bye products are accepted as inevitable. So also, scrap, discards, some waste, re-work, return, effluents, etc. It is a common belief that cutting pollution is just an expensive cost. Re-examination and value-based action can turn them into better profit earners.

7. **Giving more for less cost.**

$$\text{Value} = \frac{F\uparrow\uparrow}{C} \quad \text{or} \quad \frac{F\uparrow\uparrow}{C\downarrow} \tag{5.3}$$

Traditionally, companies use economies of scale to make and deliver highly differentiated products and services at the lowest possible costs. Alternative product (or service) concepts, alternative technologies, alternative activities, alternative function(s), alternative channels, alternative distribution mechanisms, and so on, that cost less: there are many more ways to accomplish the same objective.

Value increases with augmented products, offering more than the generic and expected product. However, this requires care in choice and coordination. For, elements that go to augment the product are interdependent. Choice of one element often dictates other elements and the levels of customer satisfaction. In addition, introducing frequent improvements disrupts smooth functioning of the system.

Example: Tooth pastes (as augmented product) now offer five additional benefits to the customer - anti-cavity and anti-gingivitis protection, better breath around the clock, plaque removal, and tartar control, in addition to cleaning teeth.

Lean manufacturing is doing more for less.

8. Giving more for small increases in cost.

$$\text{Value} = \frac{F\uparrow\uparrow\uparrow\uparrow}{C\uparrow} \tag{5.4}$$

Similar to 7 above, but where small increases in cost is translated into great increases in utility.

Like what Volkswagen did. It went on adding a gasoline gage, synchro mesh on all gears, more power to engine, locks for both doors, without large increases in price. This shows how small increases in cost can translate into great increases in utility.

9. Give a total value offering with a key benefit and threshold benefits on others.

Develop a few core competencies that give the company best-in-world capabilities in a few areas critical to the customers. Core competencies are akin to roots of a tree; and products (or services), the fruits. They emphasise technological and production expertise at specific areas. They add value. Offer the key benefits that reflect operational excellence or product leadership and keep on improving that technical and technological advantage, so as not to lose out to competition. Simultaneously, aim to manage adequate performance level in threshold functions. The total value offering should meet or exceed the customer expectations.

Honda's core competency is their small engines and power trains. Their product range includes cars, lawn mowers, garden tractors, marine engines and generators. Komatzu concentrated on quality, achieved world standards and won the Deming prize in 3 years. It continued to maintain this lead, while rationalising product development speed and attainment of variety at low cost. Each layer of advantage provided the foundation for the next.

10. Adding value not only to products, but also to customers.

Search purposefully for what is of "value" to the customers.

Traditional industrial pattern follows Benjamin Franklin's dictum: "If you invent a better mouse trap, the world will beat a path to your door." Industries have not dwelled any deeper, to find out, what makes it better, or for whom.

McDonald studied what value meant to the customers – quality and uniformity of product, speed of service, absolute cleanliness and friendliness. They designed their products to offer these values and geared their process to execute the job.

A company's strength is the knowledge of its customers' needs and its ability to fulfil those needs effectively and well. What is known covers only the articulated needs, which are about 25 percent of the total needs (including unarticulated and unserved needs and unexploited opportunities). Take time to thoroughly understand what the customers really want. They may not say it. They may forget to say it. They may articulate poorly, or may not define it well. They may not give all details. They may not wish to give all details, or may be withholding information. They may like to avoid embarrassment - looking silly or foolish. Often so adaptive in getting around problems with the product or service, they may have forgotten the problem and how they solved it. They may even have no independent ideas to offer. That is, until probed or pursued. The leading edge companies seek to fully understand and effectively meet all the latent needs of the customers.

Target activities that will make the biggest impact in customer perceived value and areas that will make the most difference to them. Because, perceptions are dynamic; and they change over time.

Apple designs its computers specifically to suit the needs of graphic designers; Sun Micro Systems, design engineers.

British Airways added an arrival lounge at London terminal, where time-stressed, travel weary businessman, arriving from USA, could freshen up quick, to go straight to their business meetings.

11. Cultivate relationships to better exploit resources, expertise and strengths.

Successful companies find opportunities to partner with organisations that possess superior skills in specific areas. They make them partners for prosperity. They believe that own success will depend on the success of customers, suppliers and channels, who can substitute for performing activities in the company value chain. A partner with skill superior to its own in that link of value chain enables creation of superior performance - economic and service - of value to the customers.

Corning, the unchallenged glass and glass-ceramics specialist, is involved in almost 50 alliances. The alliances have enabled it to capture higher value links of its business: the greater profit margins of laboratory services as opposed to least profitable glassware supply. Also, to improve economics: by diversifying into high demand products (fiber optics, consumer house wares, silicone, etc.); gaining access to markets (coming TV tubes to Asia); and extending its business (Cormetech and speciality materials).

Anywhere that different companies use similar resources, there are opportunities for reducing costs through sharing information.

12. **Cultivate speciality niches, developing high skills.**

A.T. Cross specialises in high quality pens - not throw away ballpoints or plastic felt tips.

EXTERNAL VALUE, CHAIN

Most companies control the internal links of its value chain, leaving almost all external links to others. These external links also form value chains - like customers value chain, suppliers value chain, channel value chain and stake holder value chain. Figure 5.3 shows the linkages.

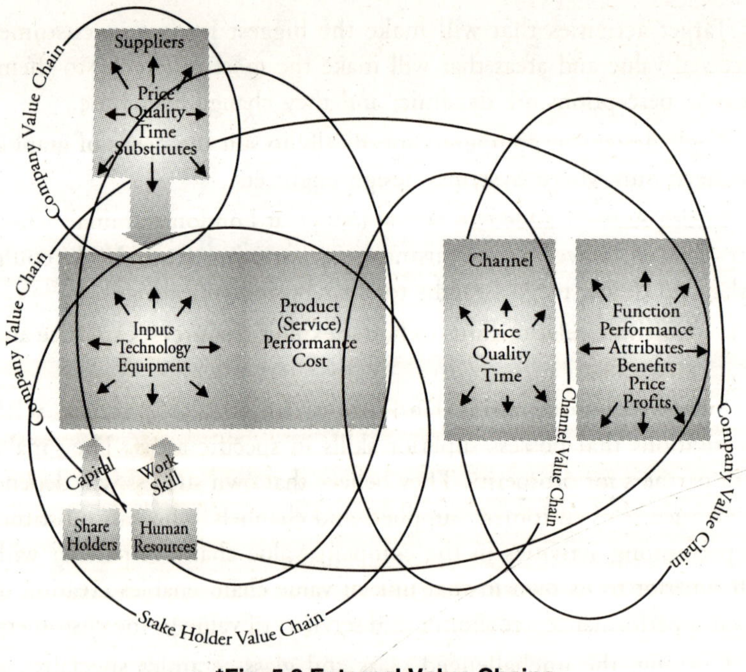

***Fig. 5.3 External Value Chains**

*(*See coloured presentation at the end of the chapter)*

By analysing all the links, the existing total value proposition and value chain can be disaggregated. The analysis would identify the linkages among activities that are critical to value and the sources of differentiation critical to creating value for the customer. It will also help to identify how, by whom, and under what conditions these can create new or better value. Every impact, interconnection and influence represents a possible opportunity for reconfiguration. The modification and reconfiguration could raise product (or service) performance and capability. The reconfigured design, attributes and features could match quality, reliability and effectively meet customer needs. It could secure dramatic reduction in time, risk and cost. It could help integrating effectiveness with efficiency in the employment of men and resources to garner unprecedented levels of performance, involvement and commitment. It could guard against unnecessary frills and gold plating.

In the early days of a product's evolution, functionality does not meet fully the needs of customers. Therefore, companies focus on utilizing the best possible performance out of the product. Attention goes to interdependent internal value chains, to push the frontier of what is possible. Examples can be had from IBM, Ford, GM, RCA, Xerox, AT&T and US Steel. Companies stretch to meet the needs of the most demanding and most profitable customers. Then only they attempt to meet the needs of other customers, in less demanding tiers of the market and in smaller niches. When this happens, technological advances almost always improve product performance beyond the needs of the general customer. Only flexible products would then meet the customized needs.

Modular products offer a solution. For, they control the interdependent links in the value chain. These can be improved without redesigning everything. Also, some trade off of performance is possible, to achieve the benefit of speed and flexibility. There is a possibility of innovation of cheaper, simpler and more convenient products and services. It could also be more profitable.

CUSTOMERS' VALUE CHAIN

Every business or industry is based on a value proposition. That value proposition contains a number of elements that the company puts together and delivers to the customers. The customers purchase the value proposition to meet their needs. The goal of the company is to create and supply a value proposition that meets the customers' requirements of value. What are of value, are importantly, function, performance and cost. These pressures are shown in black arrows in Fig. 5.1 and Fig. 5.3.

Producers often misconceive what it is that the customer actually buys. They assume that what represents value to the producer - what they put together and what they propose to deliver - is equally valuable to the customer. Values and expectations the producer holds to be real are incongruous with the actual values and customer expectations. The actual values and expectations of the customer would cover his or her functional needs and functional roles, product and service attributes, psychological needs, perception, and other intangible benefits. That represents the customers' value chain.

"A firm's product eventually becomes part of its buyer's value chain," (Porter, M.E., 1985). The company's value chain and the customers' value chain are inter-linked. The customer value chain, customer perceived value chain and the value unutilised are shown in green in Fig. 5.1 and Fig. 5.3.

"Different customers buy different kinds of value," (Treacy, M., 1995). Some view a product's uniqueness as crucial. Others seek product results and trouble-free performance. Some others go for specific attributes: better life, reliability, and dependability. Some prefer more relevant product features (run like Swiss watches, precise as German machinery). While, others may attach higher weight to availability of spares, after-sales service and faster support services. Some may go after combinations, like low price and good quality; or low price and high dependability (like Briggs and Stratten small engines); or low price, speed and ease of use; etc. Some may like individual customisation (like Airborne Express). However, all will invariably demand lower prices and progression - more of everything. As seen already, by analysing the customers' value chains, a company can identify where it can specialise or focus resources to provide a material, a process or an activity for a variety of customers, at lower cost and superior performance.

Explore the various ways in which the customers' functional needs might be better met and even go a step further, to make a significant (disproportionate) contribution to customer perceived value. Customer perceived value will usually be lower than value delivered by the company (see Fig. 5.1). The customer is king. However, how many companies actually operate on this basis? UPS let the customer dictate its services, and increased logistics engineering to provide what the customer wanted: superior tracking capabilities.

No company can be the best in all things; to all people; and at the same time. Resources are limited; and so, have to be concentrated selectively. Equipment, process, layout, etc. needed to be good at one thing (say, mass production at lowest cost) would be different from that needed for another (say, variety of products and quick responses to customer request for modifications). Methods and systems may be difficult to alter, or may lose efficiencies, when changed. Customers do understand that one cannot expect superior value in every dimension from the same company. At the same time, they know that you excel in some areas. True focus in strategy should be in performing those activities, important to the customers, more effectively than others.

No product is perfect. Everything needs service. Customer relationship, how they receive service, parts supply, parts availability at right locations, etc., are other important factors that influence the value chain. Products are physical embodiments of a set of services desired by the customers. Improving on the embodied services and service skills will increase customer value. "No company can escape the need to reskill its people, reshape its product portfolio, redesign its process and redirect resources," (Prahalad, C.K., 1994). One must explore constantly alternative concepts, techniques, mechanisms, routes, channels, etc.

Under these circumstances, there is need for being selective in the efforts to enhance value.

Product leader companies use their core competency to provide unique value that it alone can provide, like, best product, (Volvo, safest car; Honda, best small engines). They "relentlessly drive themselves to deliver extra- ordinary levels of distinctive value," (Treacy, M., 1995) in that specific dimension (safety or small engines), through operational excellence, technology upgrading and concentration of resources and skills. They keep on pushing performance boundaries, continuously improving and innovating, endlessly. They would not let up on the improvement process, neither allow gained advantages to decline, nor loose out to competition at any point of time. Simultaneously, they also strive to maintain threshold standards on all other related dimensions (Volvo on engine performance, power train, acceleration, features, etc; Honda, to diversify from cars to marine engines, generators, lawn equipment, etc.). As competition would seek to raise customer expectations about what is adequate, they ensure to remain progressively more adequate in all these dimensions. Then, they exploit ways in which they combine means and end to perform ably and adequately in the remaining dimensions.

Others maintain standards in line with customer expectations. They first determine precisely what the customers value and then organise to remain "customer friendly" or "customer intimate" (Treacy, M. 1995), or to create a "customer life style," (Prahalad, C.K., 1995), delivering what the specific customer wants. Their initiatives would be to:

- Provide the best, total value solution for the customer (like Airborne Express: on time delivery with no pre conditions; Wal-Mart Supercentres that combined food and general merchandise to offer customers lower everyday prices and more conveniences).
- Cull specific, detailed and integrated customer data, tailoring to individual customer needs, customising and meeting the current and future needs. Existing value offerings can be reconfigured (like Nike products, specifically designed for athletes, racers, etc.).
- Exploit customer interface in the value chains - firm's and the customers' - for fine-tuning differentiation in product (service) concepts (like Boeing, providing different features and interiors to each purchasing Airline's requirements).
- Blend resources and skills in ways that multiply the value of the firm and the customers (like Honda providing highly valued benefits to car owners, lawn makers, farmers, etc.).
- Do everything that lowers the customers' total cost of using the firm's product or service or other buyer costs (like Loctite's anaerobic adhesives. Reduction in customer's maintenance expenses and repair costs far outweighs the premium in price).

- Accelerate the customers' critical profit generators, minimising his system's cost effectiveness (like, GE Logic Appliances Division saving reseller inventory costs. GE adopts J - I - T method of keeping reseller stocked with consignments. Reseller pays for goods only when sold).
- Attempt to become client-driven expert in the customers' business, not doing their work, but helping them to manage theirs (like Lincoln Electric. They sell welding equipment, supplies and service; but also study customers' purchase process and use cycle to search for savings out of customers' ordering, inventory processing work and administrative routine).
- Add new technology - brain behind the brow. Optimise the service chain to improve service while keeping costs down. (Like, Burger King's TV terminals in the kitchen. Chefs read incoming orders from screen - as taken at the cash registers, out front. Fewer mistakes, less waste, time saved).

"Without customer value, there is no sustainable business," (Treacy, M., 1995). Adding to their value is the sole reason for being in business. However, their values change, particularly as customers become more sophisticated (educated and capable of detecting minor differences) and their degree of understanding of future requirements increases. Therefore, the efforts of value enhancements will have to be intense, to keep pace with the changes.

SUPPLIERS' VALUE CHAIN

The value proposition of the company contains a number of elements collected and put together from suppliers, channels and employees; and delivered to the customers.

Any business is both a customer (upstream), buying supplier-values (shown in lavender in Figs. 5.1 and 5.3) for use in own business; and a supplier (downstream), providing firm's values for use by the buyer and consumer (shown in red in Figs 5.1 and 5.3).

Carefully crafted links to reliable suppliers will continue to be at least as important to business success as are intimate ties to customers. What the suppliers provide constitute 60 percent to 70 percent of the cost of the product.

The supplier value chain creates and delivers purchased inputs that the firm uses. Typical supplier linkages are quality (of supplies and service), service (frequency and timeliness of deliveries) and material handling (packaging, unit loads, delivery procedures, order processing).

Quality, dependability, timeliness and cost reside with the supplier links. How the supplier performs his activities, and its economics will determine the cost of items supplied.

Technological change would affect the supplier value chain. Working closely with the supplier, beneficial changes can be mutually developed, giving advantages to both the supplier and the firm. Skills and resources outside the company can be availed for innovation. The objective is to induce the suppliers to focus their creativity and innovation to increase the functionality and performance of their products, to create a supply chain culture of value. The company's cost reduction objective can be broken down to the subassembly and component levels; and then, transmitted to the supplier. In turn, the supplier would find ways to design and manufacture these items.

For example, differentiation can stem from procurement of higher quality material. Suppliers have the advantage of looking at a situation from the outside. Such a view would help to effect beneficial changes.

Many companies do not make continuous make or buy analysis. They assume that what was done in the past should continue. However, if closely studied and bench marked, the company's capabilities may turn out to be significantly below the suppliers' potentials. Continual reassessment and strategic outsourcing of technology intensive areas and in service activities would substantially enhance values.

A company's procurement process and the supplier's order processing are mirror images of one another. Identical information and data needed are entered in separate documents and the tasks repeated at each end. There is little coordination between the two processes. Inconsistencies, errors, misunderstanding, etc., apart, streamlining across company processes would ensure better coordination and efficiencies. And so, super values.

CHANNEL VALUE CHAIN

Shown in Fig. 5.3 in pale yellow.

For each customer-product combination, channel economies are changing in consonance with changes in buying and selling patterns.

There is also a sales and service process or a chain of activities to create awareness of the product, disseminating product information, selling, delivering and after-sales-servicing.

How these activities are performed and their economies will influence correspondingly the costs.

Previously, the design criterion for distribution systems was the most efficient way to operate it. Often, it was not necessarily the best way for the customer to order the product. Identifying the channel activities, modifying them and using channels that are most effective for the customers, value can be altered. For those activities, that one cannot do very well or most economically, partnering and working in harmony would be the best solution.

Lee Lacocca, in his autobiography, mentions that "if a problem is caught at the manufacturing plant, it might cost two-third of what it might cost to rectify at the dealer's. That is indicative of how cost escalates with channels and affects adversely the denominator of the equation for value:

$$\text{Value} \sim \frac{\text{Function}}{\text{Cost}} \text{ or } V \sim \frac{F}{C} \tag{3.2}$$

Companies spend more than half of their purchasing budget on services- more than twice as much as they spend on other categories, including raw materials and operating goods. The Center for Advanced Purchasing Studies in USA found it at 54%. Controlling this huge expenditure would find more valuable uses for the money saved.

STAKE HOLDER VALUE

This is shown in blue in Fig. 5.3.

It is common for management to think of the shareholder as the stake holder. Hence, the special concern for shareholder value and its creation.

There are actually five types of stakeholders: the customers, the employees, the suppliers, the communities and the shareholders. Evidence shows that managing for value benefits all.

Stock options, as the major component of executive compensation, was meant to make executives share holders and align their interests with that of the owners. However, the generous distribution of options have failed to motivate value-friendly behavior. Despite the SOX internal checks and other measures, many executives focus on short-term performances, at the expense of long-term growth. They tend to manage earnings with accounting gimmicks, such as over investment, under investment and stretching permissible accounting to limits. Rewarding executives for delivering superior long-term returns and superior multi-year value may correct the situation. Value creating growth is a strategic challenge and to succeed corporations must be good at developing new businesses.

Customer value comes first. Shareholder value is derived from value that is first delivered to the customers. "Customer value, shareholder wealth and employee satisfaction move in lockstep," (Treacy, M. 1985).

What are most important and beneficial to shareholders is consistency in value creation. Also important to them is the sustained value in ability to earn higher returns than competitors. The challenge of sustaining value may be easier for companies in single product lines than for companies in multi-product lines.

IMPLEMENTING VALUE MANAGEMENT

- Value Management
- Management's Role
- Introducing the Program
- Value Management, A Way of Life
- Mechanics of Value Enhancement
- Defining the Problem
- The Workshop
- Implementation
- Final Step
- Audit
- The Result

IMPLEMENTING VALUE MANAGEMENT

6

VALUE MANAGEMENT

Value Management is a way of life - for an executive, an organization and all stake holders. It is a management technique to ensure that you are ever better, right in decisions and doing the right job. It is a tool to provide a competitive edge through enhancing value-for-money for the customer.

Value Management manages all resources - men, material, machinery and equipment, money and minutes - in the most effective and efficient manner. It is universal in application - on any program, project, product, part, equipment, building, facility, contract, and so on. It covers concept, planning, design, engineering, manufacture, assembly, upkeep, servicing, storage, movement and supply channels. It seeks to improve performance, capacity, capability, reliability, safety, etc. It is as much about increasing quality performance for the same cost or less, as reducing the cost while maintaining the quality. It reduces and eliminates all unnecessary costs, hidden costs and frills and, more importantly, prevents unnecessary use of any resource.

Majority of the techniques used in value management are not new and their comprehension and application do not require an engineering degree. The newness of Value Management lies in the use of all known, available or in-house techniques and expertise as a system for developing solutions. It is team work - multifunctional and even self directed. It secures continuous and continual improvement. It is a methodology to study value, analyze value, create, add and build value, measure value that exists, compare it with value that is required, revealing the gaps that can, and should be, bridged. It assures value in all that is made and done. Value management is dynamic (not static) and can be applied to virtually any situation. It develops approach to achieve functions.

Value Management is defined in a number of ways:

European Standard (EN 1325-1) describes it as a style of management and defines it as *the wide ranging and systematic use of value techniques as a general problem solving method in a company.* The Institute for Value Management, UK, describes it as *a practical, creative, problem solving or problem seeking service which maximizes the functional value of a project by managing its development from concept to use.* The Central Unit on Procurement – HM Treasury, UK, recommends that *the philosophy and technique of Value Management provides a structural approach to the examination and development of a project, which will increase the likelihood of achieving these requirements at optimum value for money. To be successful, it must be a continuous process.* Yet another definition says *Value Management provides a structured approach using proven methods to meet share holders' expectations with the balance between performance and resources.* The Society of American Value Engineers, SAVE International, prefers *Value Engineering* (and *Value Methodology)* as an all embracing term.

The terms Value Management (VM), Value Engineering (VE) and Value Analysis (VA) are largely used interchangeably. The consensus today is to use Value Management as the global practice of value studies that include Value Engineering (product oriented), Value Analysis (project oriented), Value Criteria (procedure and standards) and Value Assurance (Validation).

Value Analysis, as originally developed by late Larry Miles, was used as an organized approach to get better value on purchased components - providing the necessary functions at the lowest costs. It was not until years later that its application was advanced to look at all manufactured components. When the US Navy Bureau of Ships adopted Value Analysis for their submarine design and *"engineered the outcome,"* they chose to call the process Value Engineering, which name stuck. Thus Value Engineering remained the popular nomenclature. Then, a little later still, its application was extended to construction and building industry. Today, it has matured as the most potent, most effective, modern management technique, successfully applied to any economic activity, on any item, any task, any function, any place and at any level - *Value Management.*

Value work is Team work. The team will have specialists in all known techniques. Their combined efforts are to enhance the value of the product or service. If the Team has an existing item, it will first tear down the item to its elements. If it is a new item, then the concept will be torn down to its elements. Data, is collected from sources as completely and accurately as possible, to establish the criterion to be achieved, to enhance the value. Function analysis, creation of alternatives, evaluation, development, investigation, etc. follows.

MANAGEMENT'S ROLE

Value is an abstract concept, not intuitively understood. Different people interpret value differently.

Most managements believe that value is everyone's responsibility; and so, a fair degree of value management will be made by the Managers and other decision makers, as a matter of routine. However, it does not happen automatically. It is only recently that management accepted that value enhancements have to be specific assignments and require training and development of concerned personnel, for attainment of value targets. Most personnel believe they add value by what they do. Few comprehend their individual impact. All are yet to realise the enormous potential they have to create value for the company and for themselves. It is, therefore, critical to make everyone understand what value is, and how each can contribute through their individual ideas, actions and decisions.

Everyone in every function must become fully involved and committed to create, build or add value. The over riding goal would be to make managing for value the way of work for everyone in the company.

As the first step, management must demonstrate its concern for, and commitment, to manage for value. Their concern should be reflected in the message to operating management. The message must be loud and clear: "Value and the success of managing for value are important to the company." To build understanding, awareness and commitment to the managing for value program, the message should reach all employees, at all levels.

Commitment may take many forms. Inter alia, it may be:

- incorporating the managing for value approach throughout the organisation;
- integrating it as a supplement and complement to the management techniques already instituted in the company;
- training and building skills in the technique - initially, all Managers and decision makers, then all key personnel, and lastly, covering every employee;
- organising and overseeing value management projects, as a routine; and appraising and appropriately rewarding accomplishments.
- A prestudy is recommended. Here the senior management can collect and clarify their thinking. It will prevent the Team from chasing every issue they fancy when working on the projects.

As a second step, management must integrate Managing for Value to merge with existing management techniques. Such integration should not pose any problem. There are many points that are common in the philosophy of managing for value and the approaches of existing practices, as the comparison with other contemporary tools and techniques, given in Table 6.1 would reveal.

Management must modify their recruitment policy. They should thereafter recruit for their entry level jobs personnel qualified in managing for value.

As the third step, management must set the stage for value work. Managing for value is a continuous, never ending journey. Continuous improvement inevitably leads to improved productivity, efficiency, effectiveness and profitability. Managing for value is a structured approach. Structured approaches unify perspectives and produce better solutions as compared to others. Synergy in action and responsibility for value and costs are inherent expectations from everyone; but seldom realised. Managing for value makes these expectations happen. People,

Table 6.1

Idea	Technique	TQM	QC	Re–Eng.	J–I–T	Ind. Eng.	Value Eng.
Involvement To Set up	Management	• (3)	• (1)	• (3)	• (1)	• (1)	• (2)
	Employees	• (3)	• (3)				• (1)
Involvement To Operate	Management			• (2)	• (2)	• (2)	• (2)
	Employees	• (3)	• (3)	• (3)	• (3)		• (3)
Who Implements Idea	Specialists	•		•	•	•	• (3)
	Employees	•	•		•		• (3)
	Consultants	•		•	•	•	
Generators	Employees		•				• (3)
	Addl. Capital	• (3)	• (1)	• (3)		• (2)	
Requires	Procedure	•	•	•	•	•	• (2)
	Training	All	Some	Many	Many	Some	Some
Areas Covered	Design	•					• (2)
	Quality	•	•				• (2)
	Service						• (2)
	Methods	•	•	•	•	•	• (2)
	Motivation						• (3)
	Cost				•	•	• (3)
Changes Affert	Work Unit		•		•	•	• (2)
	Organisation	•		•			• (2)
Other Important Features		Raises Cost affor-dab lity crisis	Job loss. Dose not motivate survivors	Requires Excellent Vendors and Employee		Raises Efficiencies Performance	Improves effictiveness, Value returns. Recognises individual effort.

Legend • Required

Weightage, (authcr's experience, in paranthesis) Scale used: 1. Min. 2. Med. and 3. Max.

by nature, want to be involved and do their jobs well. Managing for value involves everyone, to do the right jobs, excellently. Normally, the men on the jobs are considered most knowledgeable about the jobs; and when they work together, produce better results. Managing for value is both team work and individual contribution, discovering the "gems," waiting to be developed.

What is needed is the will to align all management processes and key resources to the objective. Especially, management of time. Through conflicting priorities, multiple tasks and over commitment, senior management's actual support to the value program must be real, sizable and visible. Only by integrating the concepts into day-to-day work can the program achieve its full potential.

Quick returns follow the delegation of value work to specific personnel and holding them accountable for results. It may be easier to start, initially, with a one-man facilitator. With the addition of Value Management in the curriculum of management development institutes, a trained official for the job should not be difficult to find. Otherwise, a chosen officer could be sponsored for training in external programs. He could be used to train others.

Simultaneously, management must introduce the program.

INTRODUCING THE PROGRAM

The program is better introduced with an Orientation Seminar for all Managers and decision makers. The Seminar may last a full day. Its objective would be to expose the participants to the value concept and show them cases of achievement in value creation and enhancement. Also, to familiarise them with the mechanics of value enhancement efforts. At the close of the session, those who took part, would become convinced that a formal program to manage for value would benefit the company and themselves.

Either as part of the Seminar, or separately, the participants would make a critical review of the organisation, from the value creation and delivery angle. Many suggestions would come up. Form No. MFV 1 is suggested for a starter and the answers could be reinforced with information gathered in Forms No. MFV 2 and MFV 3. Product Line Gaps would go into Form No. MFV 4 and Execution Gaps, MFV 5.

Channel details can be gathered in Form No. MFV 6. With the data so collected and based on the comparisons resulting from these data, a preliminary assessment is made on what could be, and needs to be, done. The value proposition emerges as Form No. MFV 7 and the drivers, recorded in Form No. MFV 8. An appropriate value management project could then be formulated, using Form No. MFV 9. There would be as many projects and as many Form No. MFV 9, as there are items for value study.

The next step would be to conduct one Workshop, to prove that the added technique achieves the results. The details of the structure and process for the Workshop are given separately, under the sub heading "Workshop." The projects could come from the information in the forms and the critique during the Seminar to introduce the program. Additionally, management may include items of their own choice, which may be pressing concerns for the enterprise. Recommended solutions to each project would emerge at the conclusion of each Workshop, and in a short period of one week. It may be a more profitable product, service, or activity; betterment of field performance; improvements in manufacturing; involving lower cost on items; less capital tied up in equipment or inventory; less direct or indirect labour; etc. The review at the concluding session would prompt quick approval and implementation.

VALUE MANAGEMENT, A WAY OF LIFE

With this introductory Workshop, the necessity for this additional technique would have been proven. What remains is only to merge it with the routine.

The in-house training set up may then conduct regular 40-hr. Workshops for all key personnel and decision makers in the company. The aim would be to teach the technique to all, so that it becomes a way of life for everyone in the enterprise. At the same time, the trainees would also be solving the problems enumerated during the Seminar and in the forms.

In due course, the nucleus that began to study value problems with a one man facilitator would expand. More trained personnel would be available for facilitation work. Similarly, more trained personnel would also be available for forming teams. As many teams would get automatically formed as there are problems to solve and projects to work on. Thus, it will become a way of life for the entire enterprise.

The value efforts may then be reviewed at regular routine meetings.

MECHANICS OF VALUE ENHANCEMENT

1. The item for value enhancement is chosen.
2. The Team for the value study is selected.
3. The criteria for value enhancement is decided.
4. The problem is defined.
5. The workshop is held, where the problem is put through Function Analysis, Creation, Evaluation, Investigation and Development Phases and writing of the Value Change Plan.
6. The plan is presented, discussed, approved and implemented.
7. An audit is done to verify that the expected benefits are realised.

DEFINING THE PROBLEM

Who has not got problems? Everyone! One or more, day in and day out. Wisdom is in accepting the fact and trying to solve as many as one can.

Webster defines a problem as a perplexing question proposed for solution.

If and when one is able to state the problem, it can be solved.

The value enhancement problem or project has to be recognised, isolated and defined first. Close examination, screening, sorting out, analysing all relevant and meaningful information which have a bearing on the problem will help here. Next comes the diagnosis.

The word diagnosis in Greek means *"knowing through."* In a successful diagnosis, *"you search through possibilities, casting them aside, ruling things out, until at last, there comes a sensation of a click, a locking in place and the fragments of a puzzle snap into a clear picture."*

It is equally important to make sure that the right problem is identified and defined. For, when a patient is ill, the wrong medicine can kill him. As in medicine, so in managing for value, the identification of the real problem and its clear definition are imperatives. The objective is to cure the cause and not the symptoms.

Differences in view points help to challenge implicit assumptions about situations. They help to prevent presenting a premature problem definition and possible solving of the wrong problem.

Begin the process with establishing what it is that you (and the management) want to accomplish. Look for a present item, method, process, procedure, system or practice, which can be described and whose performance, functions and cost it is desired to be improved. The problem to which managing for value should be applied (or to which it is most effectively applied) must be capable of expression in measurable terms. Sometimes, looking at what end results are wanted, can help to figure out the problem. End the process with putting it down in writing; then getting it right. A good problem statement should include what is known, what is still unknown, and what is sought. Re-state in a number of ways and pick out the most clear and concise statement.

THE WORKSHOP

PREPARATION

By now, the items for value study for the enterprise would have been known (from Form(s) No. MFV 9, the Seminar discussions and the management choices). This list would get extended over time with additions as needed.

Experience shows that best results accrue when making studies of four or five projects for Workshop. For each, the Team would consist in twenty to twenty-five members. They must be both familiar, and connected with, the projects under study. It would be better to exclude the original designer in the item; but include a lay person, who does not know anything about it. The essential qualification for doing value work and the talent mix have been given in the companion book Value Engineering – A How to Manual. It is conventional to have representatives from finance, purchasing and industrial engineering. The team would elect their leader and facilitator. Usually, the former would be the one who has the problem or who seeks the solution.

A beginning could be made with the group that does the first Workshop, until more personnel get trained. In any case, the first few sessions in the Workshop would be a refresher in value work, explaining the reasons for poor value and setting the ground rules. The relevant hand outs for the refresher are given in the Appendix. A Project Work Book would be needed to record every thing that relates to the item under study during the Workshop and to recommend the proposed change plan. A sample Work Book is also given in the Appendix.

JOB PLAN

The Workshop follows the general route taken for Value Engineering Job Plans. The Job Plan is described in detail in the companion book – *Value Engineering - a How to Manual.*

In brief, the project (or the problem defined) is progressed through the following phases (see Fig. 6.1):

- Function Analysis
- Creation
- Evaluation
- Investigation
- Development

Function Analysis is the key to any value effort. Value being a relationship between **Function** and **Cost**, it can be enhanced by either improving the function or by decreasing the cost. Function Analysis examines the item from both angles. The Basic and Support Functions of the project (or the problem defined) and the constituent elements thereof are defined, classified, evaluated and creatively refined. The function is stated in a two word, verb-noun combination, the former to indicate the action the item performs and the latter, what is acted upon or the object of the action. Meaningful costs per function are also determined.

In the Creation phase, creative ideation techniques are used to generate a multitude of ideas, products, processes, methods, etc., to accomplish the defined functions, reliably and well. A quantity of ideas are blasted and generated creatively, suppressing the judicial faculty of the brain, and looking to provide for the functions solely as defined by the two word combination.

Refining, evaluation and ranking for cost follow in the Evaluation phase. They are then investigated (in the Investigation phase) for satisfying fully - technically and otherwise - all the requirements. Creating, evaluating, investigating, iterating when new facts are found while working these phases, finally a satisfactory value enhancement plan is derived. This is schematically shown in Fig. 6.1. Solutions are developed (in the Development phase) using the best first, then the next best and so on, in that order, using a building block approach.

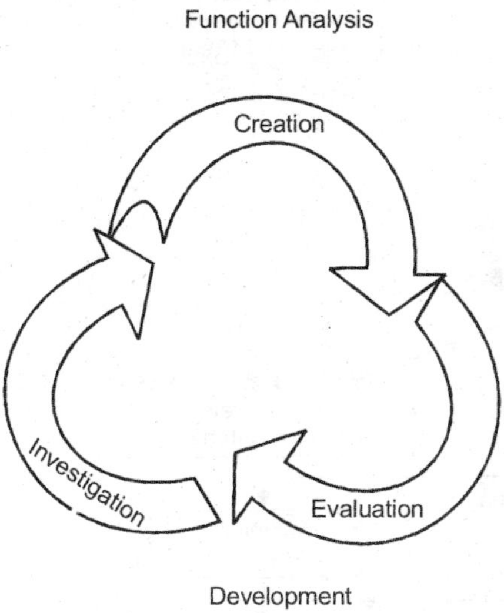

Fig. 6.1

The logic of the value effort would be evident from Fig. 6.2.

The change plan is presented at the conclusion of each Workshop. The plan would be subject to critique by all concerned and approval by the decision-maker.

IMPLEMENTATION

The actual time frame for implementation depends on the type of company, its organisation, receptivity to change, information base and complexity of the project. True realisation of value would come from company wide involvement and improved decision making; which, in turn, are predicated upon total implementation of the managing for value program.

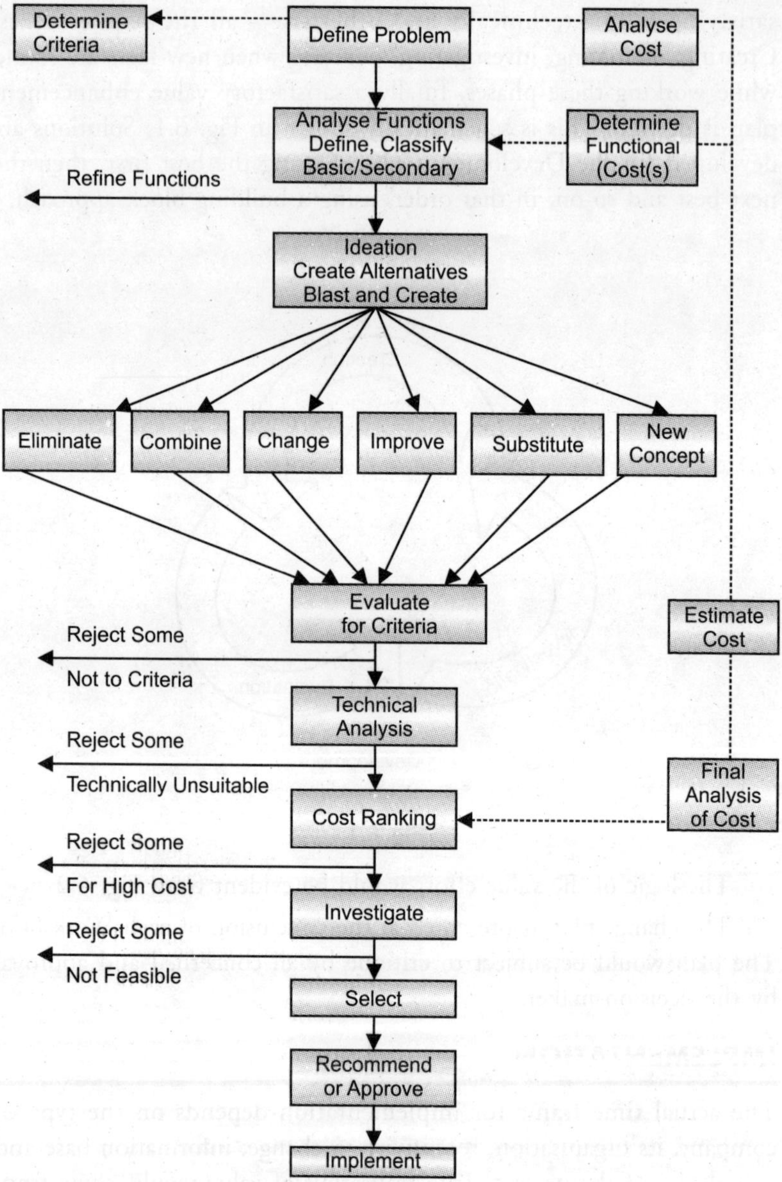

Fig. 6.2 Logic of Managing for Value

Realistic estimation of implementation costs would help in the long run to develop confidence in the value change proposals. The same caution is relevant for estimating time required for implementation. Besides, it would be prudent to drop projects that show marginal savings, although such instances may be rare. Identification of risk and all other disadvantages associated with the change and declaring them candidly are also important. How likely something would go wrong and what would happen if it did go wrong, should also be clarified.

The installation of a new idea and the introduction of any change would present human problems. So, it would be wisdom to anticipate discouragement, set backs and disappointments. By being ready for them, it would afford the choice of making a new approach. Offering a first choice and an alternative preempts the risk of rejection. Besides, it gives the decision maker his prerogative to have the last word.

If the team leader was the one who had the problem that was put to value study, he would be glad it was solved and implement it.

The progress of implementation may be reviewed and monitored until completion.

Acknowledgement of assistance taken would not only be a matter of courtesy, but also an investment for future help when needed. Recognition and appropriate rewards to all concerned would be great motivators.

FINAL STEP

The final step would be to train all key personnel so that they will manage for values on their own jobs, as routine. Thus, the technique would become a way of life with all of them.

AUDIT

Last, but not the least, is the audit of the benefits and savings realized by an independent authority. The proof of the pudding is in the eating. So also in Value Management. The proof of a good job done would be in realizing the benefits and savings estimated in the study. If it is substantiated by an independent audit, it would add to the credibility of the study. Lessons from the audit findings would go to enhance the quality of future value studies.

THE RESULT

When it becomes a way of life with all in the company, the ultimate result would certainly be better value for the company and the customer.

For, value was determined by a clear understanding of the function or functions a customer needs. Good value was created by ensuring that the item has the appropriate performance and cost. It provides the quality, reliability and esteem features that the item requires to perform effectively and well. It has just right, neither more, nor less, in everything.

Anything can be value analysed. However, of prime importance is the return for the time and resources invested. Performing an intense, detailed study on all items, concentrating on each until a factual specific proposal or alternative approach is developed, has paid rich dividends to many organisations. It has motivated positive action throughout the organisation.

GE claims $ 25 saved for each dollar spent on the value enhancement programs. Hughes Aircraft claims $ 17 and RCA, $ 15. SAVE's survey of 26 projects showed that the benefits average $ 27 saved for every dollar spent.

Value efforts are mandatory in USA for some States and the Department of Defense, Highways, Education, etc. Over half of the Fortune 500 Corporations use value studies as a matter of routine. Joy Manufacturing Company reported that, on their world-wide operations, they obtained handsome returns: 3 to 1 in the first few years of application to 24 to 1 on maturity. A minimum average return of 10 to 1 is common. Percentage cost improvement per item ranged from a low of 5 percent to a high of 73.8 percent. Many Japanese firms attribute their success to value efforts: like Matsushita, 1.6 percent of their sales and Hitachi, over 5.5 percent. A rule of thumb is that savings of 2 to 5 percent of gross sale can easily come from value efforts.

What industry needs is a technique to make people, as they are, to produce consistently good products and services of value. The key is how to make them more effective. For this, what would be ideal than Managing for value, an exercise of the very talent that one is born with - the sense of value.

Make *Managing for Value* a way of life and the future, bright and secure.

Points Worth Remembering

Rs
Managing for Value

POINTS WORTH REMEMBERING 7

- Little in industry stays constant or proprietary for long. Not products, processes, technologies, nor strategies. Neither features, nor formulae. The trend is to copy, emulate, duplicate, match, reverse-engineer or replicate.
- All actions taken will reach a threshold - a point of diminishing returns. Beyond it, further improvements will be of reduced or zero value. For example, further cost reduction may mean a sacrifice in differentiation. Choose what is of ultimate benefit and resolve the trade off.
- Narrow focus leads to myopia. Keep goals in sharp focus. Set bench marks, attain them and surpass them. Persevere.
- There would be several temptations - like: to over price; cut costs by providing less than superior service, or under-servicing; preserving the past; and exploiting innovation at the expense of value. Resist and avoid them.
- As a rule, it is not good enough to offer the same product (or service) at lower cost. There has to be something that distinguishes it from what already exists: say longer, shorter, smaller, bigger, heavier, lighter, stronger, weaker, cheaper, more expensive, different distribution system, etc.
- Differentiate between customers who represent revenues and profits and who represent only costs. Create life-time-value with

the former. The idea differentiates your company from your competitors. The strategy gives wings to the idea so that your company can soar. The value keeps your company flying high.

- Every business or industry is based on a value proposition. Present your value proposition creatively. Increase customer perception of your value offerings. Improve or find new, useful applications of existing products and services.
- The proliferation of many different management styles and techniques have bewildered industry. The dilemma of choice apart, there is considerable duplication of efforts, improper applications and retraining needs. It will be seen that value is central to many of the techniques. Managing for value will be the prescription for integration.
- Value planning will focus the critical input, "strategic intent," into the company's planning. Function analysis, FAST diagrams, Dysfunction analysis, Affinity and Tree diagrams, etc., will bring out key issues that bolster core competencies. Customer-oriented process concept will ensure that product design is customer driven, (and not producer driven). It will ensure producing a product "on the first try" that has high end-user value. It will go to eliminate redesign and/or post introduction problem solving. Management of the complex trio of activities - product design, manufacturing and factory design - will benefit considerably from Value Engineering, combined with other techniques, like QFD, DFMA, JIT, MRP, TQM, Bench Marking, Technical Road Mapping, etc. So also, policy planning, new product and service concept and delivery.
- Value based management will be the answer for all the critical strategic issues of the future - timing, quality, flexibility, innovation and excellence.

APPENDIX

Knowledge, technology
are at the core of
everything—
everything of Value

- Business Realites – A Comparison
- Forms
  - From Number MFV 1 – Diagnosis of Current Business
  - From Number MFV 2 – Your Uniqueness
  - From Number MFV 3 – Product Line Gaps
  - From Number MFV 4 – Growth
  - From Number MFV 5 – Execution Gaps
  - From Number MFV 6 – Channels
  - From Number MFV 7 – Value Proposition
  - From Number MFV 8 – Drivers in the Value Chain
  - From Number MFV 9 – Project Summary

Business Realities—A Comparison

	Then	Now
Company	Win by bigness, superiority of location, uniqueness, proprietary nature.	Win by excellence: leadership due to product excellence.
	Aims for leadership as sole supplier.	Aims to supply more of whatever the customer buys.
	Efficiency in what they do.	Efficiency combined with effectiveness.
	Conform to open or national standards.	Conform to International standards.
	Trade in domestic markets.	Trade globally, including domestic markets.
	Concerned with only own success.	Committed for customer success (reflected as own success).
Management	Manage from top, down.	Manage up and down and across.
	Militaristic, discipline and control.	Participative, leading and mentoring.
	Dominate and go it alone.	Collaborate and network with others.
	Departments for each specialty.	Teams, preferably self-directed.
	Improve, using internally generated measures.	Improve by bench marking best in line of business and best in everything.
	Seek and solve cost intensive problems.	Seek and solve revenue intensive opportunities.
	Increase efficiency of effort.	Increase effectiveness of efficient effort.
	Product centered, sustaining competitive advantage.	Customer centered, inventing new advantages.
	Speed and streamline individual tasks.	Coordinate and control entire system.

Contd....

Product (or Service)	Mass produced.	Mass customised, with common platforms.
	Standard, uniform.	Personalised, variety.
	Self designed and styled.	Designed and developed with customers.
	Conservatively developed.	Quick, concept to product.
	Best in quality.	Best quality per cost.
	Most prestigious.	Most functional.
	Core product.	Augmented product.
	Turn multi performer, adding features.	Find new applications of existing product.
	Focus on product and service.	Focus on value chain.
	Continuing existing product or service as such.	Introducing a steady steam of new products or of improvements to existing products.
Supplier	Make everything. Buy least.	Outsource non-core items.
	Use multiple sources of supply.	Use few suppliers.
	Go to only registered parties.	Form alliances with the best.
Customer	Lowest in price.	Best value for the money.
	Accept what company can make.	Make, supply what is needed by customers.
	Get feed back for post-introduction problem solving.	Designing with customers, pre-empting problems for use.
	Customer to afford company offerings.	Customer to become unable to afford doing without your value offering.
	All customers treated alike.	Create life time value with customers representing revenues and profits.
Marketing	Sell product (or service) to customers.	Sell value to customers
	Mass marketing.	Target marketing.
	Serve markets.	Serve and create markets.
	Meet customers' expectations.	Exceed customers' expectations: even create a need.
	Sales as one time transaction.	Sales as a continuing relationship.

Project		*Ref. No.*	
		Date	

Diagnosis of Current Business

Item	*Today*	*Estimate*	
		5 years later	*10 years later*
Your Products			
Related Products			
Your Markets			
Related Markets			
Your Cost			
Your Margins			
Your Customers			
How reached			
Your Competitors			
Your Special Skills or Capabilities			
Your Competitive edge (what is your differentiation)			

MFV1

Project *Ref. No.*

Date

Your Uniqueness

Item	*Today*	*Estimate*	
		5 years later	*10 years later*
Technology Equipment Process Materials Treatment Other (specify)			
What is the remaining Potential. Technology Equipment Process Other (Specify)			
Estimate to close the gap Technology Equipment Process Other (Specify)			

Preliminary Assessment:
(What is wrong and what could be done to correct)

Project *Ref. No.*

Date

Product Line Gaps

Comparison Item	*Years*	*Competitors*		
Technology				
Equipment				
Process				
Design				
Materials				
Features				
Skills				
Number of Assemblies				
Number of Sub-assemblies				
Number of Parts				
Number of Fasteners				
Number of Mating Surfaces				
What You Make				
What You Buy				
Changes Made, What and When				
The speciality				
Anything additional				
Does Your Total Value Offering Match the Customer's Needs				
Where Different and How				
How to fill the gap or mismatch Your ideas				

MFV 3

Project	*Ref. No.* *Date*

Growth – 5 to 10 years' Data

Item	*Details*	
	Yours	*Competitors*
Revenue		
Profits		
Profit margin per product (Specify)		
Cost per product (Specify)		
Your unprofitable products		
Your unprofitable markets		
Are you growing in the best segments		
If not, what hinders growth		

What needs to be done to reverse:

Technology	
Equipment	
Method	
Materials	
Design	
Process	
Skill	
Training	
Others (Specify)	

MFV 4

Project	*Ref. No.*
	Date

Execution Gaps

Comparison Item	*Details*
How old is the technology	
What changes were made and when	
Is there any breakthrough new technology	
Is any imminent	
Is your key process customer oriented	
Is your customer's key process matched to your product/process	
What and where is the difference	
What will it need to fill this gap:	☐ Equipment ☐ Skill ☐ Process ☐ Others (specify)
Performance:	☐ Productivity ☐ Yield ☐ Cost ☐ Others (specify)
What will it need to improve:	☐ Productivity ☐ Yield ☐ Cost ☐ Other (Specify)
Are you measuring your performance against customer targets:	☐ Customer needs ☐ Customer costs ☐ Customer productivity ☐ Customer quality
Are you allocating resources to improve:	☐ Customer needs ☐ Customer costs ☐ Customer productivity ☐ Customer quality

(Contd...)

Your management techniques and controls: Changes made

Where	*What*	*When*
Organisation		
Production		
Planning		
Scheduling		
Control		
Performance Analysis		
Safe Working Practices		
Make or Buy Decisions		
Engineering changes		
Inspection/Testing		
Scrap/Rework		
Others (specify)		

MFV 5

Project *Ref. No.*

Date

Channels

The channels you use

The channels used by competitors

Differences:

☐ Price ☐ timeliness ☐ frequency ☐ lot sizes ☐ packaging

☐ safety ☐ warranty ☐ tractability ☐ others (specify)

Could you use/adapt them to improve your offerings tot he most valuable market segments

What benefits will accrue

How will it affect your offerings to remaining segments

Do your customers prefer them

What modifications are needed

Is modification feasible

What benefits will it yield

MFV 6

Project | Ref. No.
Date

Value Propostion

Item	*Yours*	*Competitors*	
Your total Value Propostion			
Particular Product or Service			

Where and what is the difference:

Price

Design

Life

Quality

Realiability

Features

Attributes

Properties

Composition

Material

Treatment

Service

Warranty

Returns

Functions:

Primary or Basic

Secondary

Support

MFV 7

Project *Ref. No.*

Date

Drivers in the Value Chain

Difference in Value chain:

- ☐ Market Research
- ☐ Product Design
- ☐ Process Design
- ☐ Logistics
- ☐ Quality Control
- ☐ Equipment
- ☐ Materials
- ☐ Treatment
- ☐ Skill
- ☐ Training
- ☐ Warehousing
- ☐ Distribution
- ☐ Post Sale Service
- ☐ Manuals
- ☐ Warranty
- ☐ Advertising
- ☐ Others (specify)

Item	*Details*
Your core skill:	
Do you have everything to excel here	
How can the gap be filled	
Your threshold skills in the value chain	
How does this compare with the competition	
Is there any activity in your value chain that can be done upstream or downstream	
Can any activity be changed to improve value chains upstream/downstream	
Your Value Proposition:	
Does it match all Customer Needs and Requirements	
What project would improve, to fill the gaps or correct mistakes	

MFV 8

Project	*Ref. No.*
	Date

Project Summary

1. Purpose of the project	
2. Expected completion	
3. Approving authority	
4. Scope of project	
5. What is not included in the project	
6. Project item described	
7. Market Country	
Segment	
User	
8. Life cycle of item	
9. Project assumptions	
10. Project constraints	
11. Possible trade off	
12. Make or buy policy	
13. Distributors	
14. Suppliers Distributors	
Dealers	
Retailers	
Distributors	
Customer Needs	
Must have	
Good to have	

MFV 9

WORKSHOP HAND OUT

- **Persons for Poor Value**

  Lack of Information.

  Lack of Ideas.

  Lack of Time.

  Lack of Attention.

  Lack of Listening.

  Lack of Problem Ownership.

  Lack of Experience.

  Poor Quality

  Honest Wrong Beliefs.

  Habitual Thinking

  Risk of Personal Loss.

  Reluctance to Seek Advice

  Habits and Attitudes.

  Unrealistic Requirements.

  Temporary of Changed Circumstances.

  Changing Technology.

  Poor Communications.

  Prejudice

  Misconceptions.

  Desire to Conform.

  Poor Interaction Among Contributing Disciplines.

  Creep.

  Non-Value-Adding Work.

  Waste.

- **Ground Rules for Value.**

Ground Rules for Value

1. Value is utility measured against price.

   A product is the tangible object a customer buys. A service is the intangible result of the efforts of someone-else.

   They both provide some benefits or returns, desired by the customer to meet a need, or to solve a problem.

   The customer pays a price in exchange for the product or service.

2. A product or service with the right attributes for the needs will be of value to the customers.

   What a product is, what it does and what it costs, are matters of fact. What it should be, what it should do, what improvements can be made, and what it should cost are matters of value. High speed and low speed, large size and small size, high cost and low cost are matters of fact. The right speed, right size and right cost are matters of value.

   When right is understood for a given purpose, you hit the point of golden balance.

   Anything more will be wasteful. Anything less will be unacceptable.

3. Value can be enhanced through accumulation of several small changes, appropriate to cater to customer needs.

   Product attributes, features, service characteristics, performance, life, technology employed, quality of inputs, skill and experience used, information used to control, redesigning, degree of complexity–all these and many more, there are several avenues to change.

Any change in any of these influences performance, costs and the basis of differentiation–which in totality is value.

4. The value change of any enhancement will depend on its additional merit (use, perfor- mance) and difference in cost.

   Enhancing the attributes or features will raise the value of the product or service, only if such enhancement in attributes and features are beneficial and necessary.

5. What the attributes and features are, and in what quantity, quality, mix, combination or configuration these are present, will determine the cost of the product or service, and the differentiation with competitve offerings.

   If the added cost results in a performance level not otherwise attainable, and this performance level makes the product better in whatever way the customer wants, the value is increased. If not, and if the performance exceeds the rquirements of its application, the value is lowered.

6. The goal is to create, produce and supply value (product or service) for the customers that exceed the cost.

7. Value is value in use: the way the customers use you, your product or service in their operations. Customer value is in the set of benefits sought. Often there is a core need, some primary, over riding requirement, or desire for accomplishment or satisfaction. There may be a series of additional, supplementary needs: the product or service must present a best value solution to the core need. The degree of satisfaction may vary. The attributes and features in the product or service may mix and match the supplementary needs in different combinations and provide at least threshold values.

8. Value results from the customers' perception of the total satisfaction provided by the product or service. That perceived difference, between one product (component or brand) and another, enables the customer to decide to purchase. This difference is due, partly to scientific reasoning (as in price, Performance, function, life, reliability, etc. Quantifiable items).

It is also influenced by abstract forces - something imagined, and something emotional (as in liking, aesthetics or esteem, color, shape, style, configuration, etc. Non quantifiable).

9. Value is knowing and applying one's product and service to generate revenues and profits for the customers.
10. Value should be the criteria for investments and resource allocation, share and priorities.
11. Value is a relationship, established by comparison. It is about performance compared to needs; intent compared to performance; product compared to price; feature or attribute compared to satisfaction; and so on.

    Value enhances with increasing performance, if and ony if, the customer needs, wants, and is willing to pay for more performance.

    Company performance, product performance and service performance are measured in terms of value added.
12. The value of a product or service depends on controllable internal factors. Which are materials (functional ability, producibility, reliability), performance (basic or primary function), methods (secondary or support function), and procedures of production and execution, design specification, skill, expertise, etc.
13. Value also depends on applied situation, external to the company. Which are channels and logistics, competition, market demand, vagaries of the supplier, needs of the customer, etc.
14. Value is the lowest cost at which a function, by any means, can be accomplished effectively, reliably and well.
15. Customer value lies in his or her critical success factors.

PROJECT WORKBOOK FOR VALUE STUDIES

Project	*Ref. No*
	Date:

Details of item to be studied:

Data package to accompany:

Relevant ❑ Layout ❑ Sketches ❑ Specifications ❑

Performance Requirements ❑

Operation Sheets ❑ Standard Practice Sheets ❑ Flow Charts ❑

Cost Data ❑

Safety Requirements ❑

Support and Test Requirements ❑

Physical and Environment Requirements ❑

Others:

A Model, An Assembly, One Set of all parts.

VALUE STUDY PROJECT

Project	*Ref. No*
	Date:

THE TEAM

NAME	DESIGNATION	TELE. NO.
TEAM LEADER		
TEAM MEMBERS		

OTHER TO BE CONSULTED
Engineering/Production
Purchasing/Quality Control
Estimation
Customers
Specialists
Suppliers

ANYTHING CAN BE VALUE ENHANCED

Project	*Ref. No*
	Date:

INFORMATION PHASE

DESCRIBE THE PROJECT FOR VALUE STUDY	Present procedure, design, system preformance requirements, criteria. (What is it ?)

OBJECTIVES OR REQUIRED CRITERIA – NOT TO BE COMPROMISED (What does it do ?)

DESIRED CRITERIA OR FEATURES – Subject to trade off and optimisation DESIRABLE, BUT NOT ESSENTIAL

USE GOOD HUMAN RELATIONS

Project	*Ref. No*
	Date:

INFORMATION PHASE

Cost,
Quantities,
Time,
Other Indicators.

Reference/Source	Abstract of Data

BE FACTUAL AND SPECIFIC

Project	*Ref. No*
	Date:

LISTS OF DOCUMENTS

(Lists all books, periodicals, technical journals, documents, specifications, and drawing, etc., used for information abstracted in the Workbook).

FACTS FROM RELIABLE SOURCES

Project	Ref. No
	Date:

ESSENTIAL DATA

Identify the Project Product ( ) Assembly ( )
Part ( ) Service ( )

Scope of Study

1. What is it expected to do?
2. What are the most significant features?
3. What is the state of development?

Quantities and Product Life

1. Where is the item used?
2. How many are used?
3. Where else can the item be used?
4. How many are produced now?
5. How will it be produced over the next two years?

Marketing Requirements

1. Is this what the customer *really* wants today?
2. What are the customer's desires?
3. What may he want tommorrow?
4. What will *contribute most* to sales?

Greater Safety	( )	Greater Reliability	( )
Improved Performance	( )		
Added Capability	( )	Improved Apperance	( )
Easier Maintenance	( )		
Lower Overall Cost	( )	Lower Sale Price	( )

IDEAS ARE KEY TO SUCCESS

SO, SEARCH THE GLOBE

Project	*Ref. No*
	Date:

TO ANALYSE VALUE OF TIME

Timeliness as OPPORTUNITY

Earliest Feasible Starting Date

Most Timely Starting Date

Deadline

Cost of timely Start

Value of Timely Start

Timing for the BEST SEQUENCE

Must Precede

Be Concurrent With

Must Follow

Cost of Right Sequence

Value of Right Sequence

Time as DURATION

Working Days Required

Starting Date

Completion Date

Cost of Completing on Time

Value of Completing on Time

Setting PRIORITIES

Should be Done Before

Concurrent With

Should Follow

Total Cost

Economic Value

Strategic Value

Risk in Doing the Job

Risk in Not Doing the Job

VERIFY AND VALIDATE

Project	*Ref. No*
	Date:

FUNCTION DEFINITION

Assembly: ____________________

Drawing No: ____________________

Basic Function: ____________________

NO.	PART	FUNCTION(S)		FUNCTIONAL		LEVEL ASSY.		REMARKS
		VERB	NOUN	BASIC	SECOND	BASIC	SECOND	

YOU NEED THEM FAST AND YOU NEED THEM RIGHT

Project	*Ref. No*
	Date:

FUNCTION CLASSIFICATION

Function being considered			
Logic Question: IF WE ELIMINATE Will it do the job for which it was made?			
Answer (Choose one) **NO** **YES, it could**			
If NO, BASIC **If YES, SECONDARY**			

FUNCTION THE HEART OF VALUE IS ENGINEERING

Project	Ref. No
	Date:

FUNCTION CLASSIFICATION

Approaching from the point of view of *USE*

Item	Function Definition

DEFINE FUNCTION IN TWO WORDS: ACTION VERB AND MEASURABLE NOUN

Project	*Ref. No*
	Date:

FUNCTION CLASSIFICATION

Approaching on the basis of *PARTS*

Item	Functional Unit	Function Definition

LOOT AT THE FUNCTION NOT THE ITEM OR PART

Project	Ref. No
	Date:

FUNCTION CLASSIFICATION

Defining on the basis of *CHARACTERISTICS*

PART:

RAW MATERIAL:

PHYSICAL PROPERTIES:

CHEMICAL PROPERTIES:

PROCESSING/MACHINING:

TREATMENT:

KEEP FUNCTION DEFINITION SIMPLE

Project	*Ref. No*
	Date:

FUNCTION CLASSIFICATION

Assembly Dwg. No. ______________________

Drawing No. ______________________

KEY LETTER	FUNCTION	WEIGHT
A		
B		
C		
D		
E		
F		
G		
H		
I		
J		
K		

	B	C	D	E	F	G	H	I	J	K	TOTAL
A											
B											
C											
D											
E											
F											
G											
H											
I											
J											
K											

SCALE:

1. MINIMUM DIFFERENCE
2. MEDIUM DIFFERENCE
3. MAJOR DIFFERENCE

FUNCTION: A WANT TO SATISFY A REQUIREMENT

Project	Ref. No
	Date:

FUNCTION RELATIONSHIP

WHY	FUNCTION	HOW

DEFINE, CLASSIFY, EVALVATE, SCALE

Project	Ref. No
	Date:

THE BASIC FAST MODEL

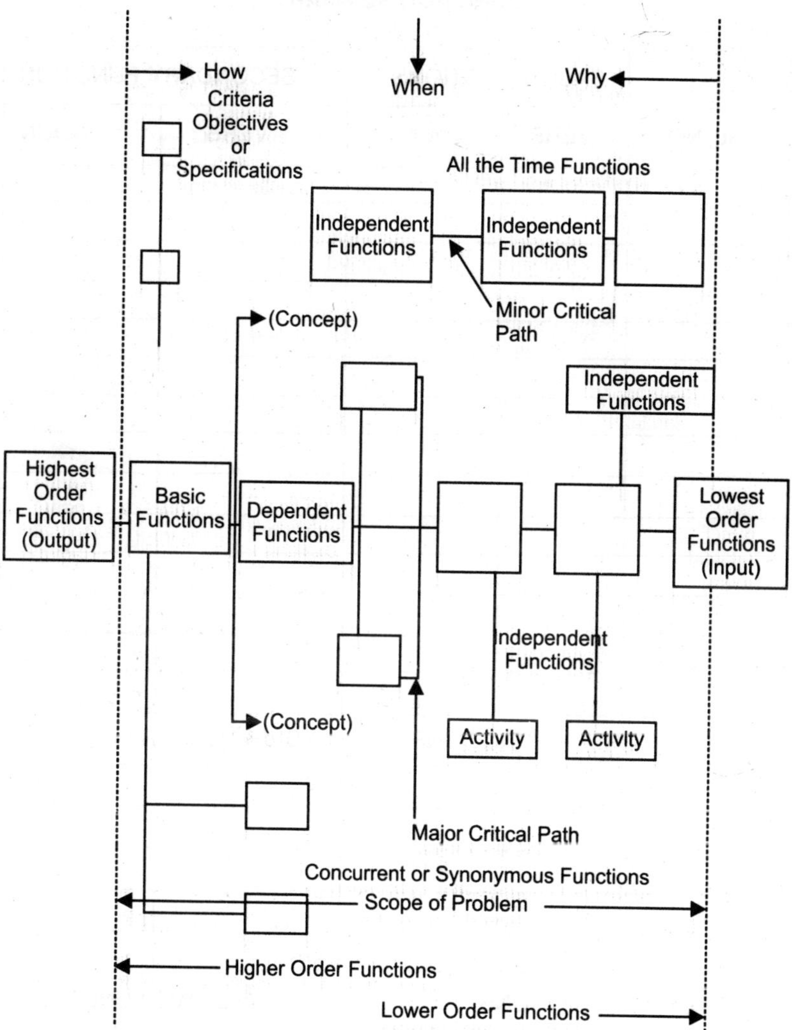

Project	*Ref. No*
	Date:

FUNCTION SUMMARY

	BASIC FUNCTIONS		SECONDARY FUNCTIONS	
SL. NO.	VERB	NOUN	VERB	NOUN
HIGHER ORDER FUNCTIONS			LOWER ORDER FUNCTIONS	
ONE TIME FUNCTIONS			ALL TIME FUNCTIONS	

FUNCTIONS IS THE HEART OF VE

Project	*Ref. No*
	Date:

COST ANALYSIS

Sl. No.	Operation Process	Cost/ Unit	Annual Cost	Function Secured or Desired	Remarks

CHECK & RECHECK TO BE SURE

Project									Ref. No Date:

FUNCTION – COST ANALYSIS

FUNCTION

Sl. No	Part	Cost per part						

CHECK : VALIDITY, ACCURACY, COMPLETENESS

Project	*Ref. No*
	Date:

FUNCTION —COST —WORTH ANALYSIS

Sl. No.	Function	Allocated Cost C	Function Worth **W**	Basis for Worth	Value Gap **C – W**	Value Index **W / C**

COST IS WHAT WE PAY, WORTH IS WHAT WE SHOULD PAY

Project	Ref. No
	Date:

CREATIVE PHASE—IDEA LISTING

	VERB	NOUN
FUNCTION		

REMEMBER, NO CRITIMISM, NO ROAD BLOCKS
MORE QUANTITY, NOT QUALITY
THE WILDER, THE BETTER

Sl. No.	IDEA
1.	
2.	
3.	
4.	
5.	
That is the spirit. You have just warmed up.	
6.	
7.	
8.	
9.	
10.	
Keep going. You are doing great	
11.	
12.	
13.	
14.	
15.	

CREATE DELIBERATELY

Project	*Ref. No*
	Date:

CREATIVE PHASE—IDEA LISTING CONTINUED

Sl. No.	IDEA
16.	
17.	
18.	
19.	
20.	
Don't give up yet. Consult the check list generate more ideas	
21.	
22.	
23.	
24.	
25.	
You can do it. You have the capacity	
26.	
27.	
28.	
29.	
30.	
One more go—Some more ideas make us proud of you.	
31.	
32.	
33.	
34.	
35.	

BLAST, CREATE, REFINE

Project		Ref. No
		Date:

IDEA COMPARISON

IDEA	ADVANTAGE	DISADVANTAGES (Note ways to overcome)	RANK

BE HONEST AND FAIR

Project	*Ref. No*
	Date:

FEASIBILITY RANKING

	A	B	C	D	Total
1.					
2.					
3.					
4.					
5.					

NOW IS THE TIME TO JUDGE

Project	Ref. No
	Date:

IDEA SELECTION WORKSHEET

BEST ALTERNATIVES					
Total Weight Factors					
Cost (Estimated)					
Weight Factor / Cost					

BE OBJECTIVE

Project	*Ref. No*
	Date:

ITEM ____

ASSEMBLY ____________________ SUB–ASSEMBLY ______________

PART ______________ QUANTITY PER YEAR ____________________

BASIC FUNCTIONS	SECONDARY / SUPPORT FUNCTIONS
PRESENT	PROPOSED
FINDINGS AND RECOMMENDATIONS	
SAVINGS	
PROJECT PARTICIPANTS	

PROPOSAL, SUPPORTED BY FACTS, IS IRREFUTABLE

Project	*Ref. No*
	Date:

FINANCIAL ASPECTS & EVALUATIONS OF CHANGE PROPOSED

COST DATA (PER UNIT)	PRESENT	PROPOSED	SAVINGS	% SAVINGS
MATERIAL COST				
LABOR COST				
OVERHEAD COST				
OTHER COST				
UNIT COST				
ANNUAL REQUIREMENTS				
TOTAL COST PER UNIT				

BE THOROUGH
RE-CHECK CALCULATIONS

Project	*Ref. No*
	Date:

LIFE CYCLE COST ANALYSIS

(i.e., owning and operating/maintaining costs during the product life cycle)

Sl. No.	Details of costs per Item	Existing Design	Proposal 1	Proposal 2
1.	Total Initial cost per unit			
2.	Annual Energy Costs of Operation: i. Power –Watts ii. Fuel Oil –Liters iii. Coal/Coke –Ton iv. Others			
	Total			
3.	Maintenance Costs per year: i. Lubrication ii. Replacements iii. Labour iv. Interest on Investment (Initial Cost) v. Others			
	Total			
4.	i. Scrap realisation expected. ii. Life expected Depreciation/year.			
	Total			
5.	Total annual Costs (add all total boxes)			
6.	Comparative Savings			
7.	Present Worth of Total LCC Saving			

CHECK ONCE AGAIN, VALIDATE YOUR ASSUMPTIONS

Project	*Ref. No*
	Date:

IMPLEMENTATION PLAN

1. How should the proposal be implemented?
2. What should be changed? In what sequence?
3. Who should do it?
4. How long should it take? Prototype: Lab. Tests: Field Tests: Review, Re-engineering. Product Go Ahead: First Lot Ready :
5. Any deadline required?
6. Implementation costs?
7. What are risks?

THE PROOF IS IN DOING IT

Project	*Ref. No*
	Date:

VALUE ENGINEERING CHANGE PROPOSAL
SUMMARY OF RECOMMENDATIONS

	PROPOSAL 1		PROPOSAL 2	
SHORT TERM				
LONG TERM				
FINANCIAL DETAILS	SHORT TERM	LONG TERM	SHORT TERM	LONG TERM
DESIGN				
PROTOTYPE				
TESTING				
DEVELOPMENT				
MAKE/BUY				
CONSTRUCTION				
INSTALLATION				
TOOLING				
RUNNING IN				
OTHERS				
TOTAL				

DECISION BY APPROVING AUTHORITY	DECISION
RECEIVED ON ____________	☐ APPROVED
CONSIDERED ON __________	☐ NOT APPROVED
NEXT REVIEW ON ___________	☐ TO RESTUDY
	☐ TO MODIFY

Date _____ Signature __________

INVEST IN THE FUTURE

Project		Ref. No
		Date:

Additional Sheet

VALUE: THE FORCE

THAT DETERMINES WHAT SURVIVES

Project	*Ref. No*
	Date:

SELECTING FEASIBLE IDEAS

Idea	Advantage	Disadvantage

LET US MAKE THINGS BETTER

BIBLIOGRAPHY

1. Miles, Lawrence D., *Technique of Value Analysis and Engineering*, 1972, Mc Graw-Hill.
2. Mudge, Arthur E., *Value Engineering-A Systematic Approach*, 1989, J. Pohl Associates.
3. Tufty, Harold G., "Compendium on Value Engineering," 1983, The Indo American Society.
4. Drucker, Peter E., *Management Tasks, Responsibilities, Practices*, 1975, Allied Publishers (P) Ltd.
5. Lala, R. M., *The Creation of Wealth*, 1981, IBH Publishing House.
6. Harrington, James H., *The Improvement Process*, 1987, Mc Graw-Hill.
7. Champy, James, *Re-engineering Management*, 1995, Harper Business.
8. Thomas, Teal, *First Person tales of Management, Courage and Tenacity*, 1996, Harvard Business Reiew Books.
9. Porter, Michael E., *Competitive Advantage*, 1985, Free Press.
10. Treacy, Michael and Wiersema, Fred, *The Discipline of Market Leaders*, 1995, Addison- Wesley Publishing Company.
11. Raven, A.D., *Profit Improvement by Value Analysis, Value Engineering and Purchase Price Analysis*, 1971, Cassell.
12. Gale, Bradley T, *Managing Customer Value*, 1994, Free Press.
13. Fallon, Carlos, *Value Analysis to Improve Productivity*, 1971, Wiley Interscience.
14. Clifford, D.K.Jr., and Cavanagh, R.E., *The Winning Performance*, 1985, Bantam Books.
15. Peters, Tom J., *Thriving on Chaos*, 1988, Alfred A Knopf.

16. Hammel, Gary and Prahalad C.K., *Competing for the Future*, 1994, Havard School Press.
17. Schlender, B.R., "*How Sony Keeps the Magic Going*," Fortune, February 24, 1992.
18. Freidman Thomas L, *The World is Fat*, 2005, Fararr, Straus and Giroux.
19. Swamy Dayananda, "*The Value of Values*," Ashra Vidya Gurukulam, Saylorsburg, 1953.
20. IW, *Industry Week*, 1991, 1992, 1996, Penton Publications.
21. *Time*, The Weekly News Magazine.

INDEX